DEVELOPING
ASSESSMENT-
CAPABLE
VISIBLE
LEARNERS

GRADES K–12

DEVELOPING ASSESSMENT-CAPABLE VISIBLE LEARNERS

GRADES K–12

MAXIMIZING SKILL, WILL, AND THRILL

NANCY FREY
JOHN HATTIE
DOUGLAS FISHER

resources.corwin.com/assessment-capable

FOR INFORMATION:

Corwin

A SAGE Company

2455 Teller Road

Thousand Oaks, California 91320

(800) 233-9936

www.corwin.com

SAGE Publications Ltd.

1 Oliver's Yard

55 City Road

London EC1Y 1SP

United Kingdom

SAGE Publications India Pvt. Ltd.

B 1/I 1 Mohan Cooperative Industrial Area

Mathura Road, New Delhi 110 044

India

SAGE Publications Asia-Pacific Pte. Ltd.

3 Church Street

#10-04 Samsung Hub

Singapore 049483

Publisher and Senior Program Director: Lisa Luedeke

Editorial Development Manager: Julie Nemer

Editorial Assistants: Jessica Vidal and Sharon Wu

Production Editor: Melanie Birdsall

Copy Editor: Diane DiMura

Typesetter: C&M Digitals (P) Ltd.

Proofreader: Eleni-Maria Georgiou

Indexer: Molly Hall

Cover Designer: Janet Kiesel

Marketing Manager: Rebecca Eaton

Printed in the United States of America

ISBN 978-1-5063-8998-1

This book is printed on acid-free paper.

SUSTAINABLE FORESTRY INITIATIVE

Certified Chain of Custody
Promoting Sustainable Forestry
www.sfiprogram.org
SFI-01268

SFI label applies to text stock

19 20 21 22 10 9 8 7 6 5 4 3

CONTENTS

Chapter 6

Assessment-Capable Visible Learners...
Monitor Progress and Adjust Their Learning   95

Chapter 7

Assessment-Capable Visible Learners...
Recognize Their Learning and Teach Others   115

Chapter 8
Mindframes of Schools That Create
Assessment-Capable Visible Learners 135

Visit the companion website at

 resources.corwin.com/assessment-capable

for videos and downloadable resources.

LIST OF VIDEOS

Note From the Publisher: The authors have provided video and web content throughout the book that is available to you through QR (quick response) codes. To read a QR code, you must have a smartphone or tablet with a camera. We recommend that you download a QR code reader app that is made specifically for your phone or tablet brand.

Videos may also be accessed at
resources.corwin.com/assessment-capable

ACKNOWLEDGMENTS

Corwin gratefully acknowledges the contributions of the following reviewers:

Kristine Allen, Teacher, Contoocook Valley School District, New Hampshire

Lynn Angus Ramos, Curriculum Coordinator, DeKalb County School District, Georgia

Lydia Bowden, Assistant Principal, Pinckneyville Middle School, Gwinnett County Public Schools, and Former Literacy Coach, High School Language Arts Teacher, and Middle School Teacher, Georgia

Jenni Donohoo, Education Consultant, Ontario Ministry of Education, Ontario, Canada

Connie Hamilton, EdS, K–12 Curriculum Director, Author, and Education Consultant, Saranac Community Schools, Michigan

Erika Tucker, PhD, English Language Arts Coordinator, Rockdale County Public Schools, Georgia

INTRODUCTION

The Foundation: Visible Learning

Since *Visible Learning* was first published in 2009, there have been many across the education field who have taken advantage of its transformative potential. The analysis of learning results from hundreds of millions of students worldwide who addressed important questions about the conditions needed for learning to occur. Far more than a "what works" list, this and the subsequent works that have followed, have constructed an explanatory story about the schooling of children and the adults who have dedicated their professional lives to advancing learning. The results reported in *Visible Learning* make it clear that when students know how to learn, they are able to become their own teachers. Termed a *visible learner* these students "exhibit the self-regulatory attributes that seem most desirable for learners (self-monitoring, self-evaluation, self-assessment, self-teaching)" (Hattie, 2009, p. 22). Do you know a visible learner when you see one?

Characteristics of Visible Learners

Visible learners

- Can be their own teacher
- Can articulate what they are learning and why
- Can talk about how they are learning—the strategies they are using to learn
- Can articulate their next learning steps

- Can use self-regulation strategies

- Seek, are resilient, and aspire to challenge

- Can set mastery goals

- See errors as opportunities and are comfortable saying that they don't know and/or need help

- Positively supports peers' learning

- Know what to do when they don't know what to do

- Actively seek feedback

- Have metacognitive skills and can talk about these skills

We see the attributes of visible learners as critical for school success and consistent with our focus on assessment-capable visible learners. In other words, ensuring that students become assessment capable is one of the implementation routes for the *Visible Learning* work. A significant aspect of the *Visible Learning* initiative has been to change the narrative from a focus on teaching to a focus on learning. Of course, teachers use strategies to ensure that students learn, but we believe that too much of the conversation is focused on what the teachers are doing rather than on the learning of the students. Instead, teaching must always be considered in terms of its impact on student learning. If a student is not progressing, educators need to know why, and what it means. In a *Visible Learning* classroom, teachers see student learning as feedback about their teaching. How could we ever expect students to set goals, develop the wisdom to use strategies to help themselves, seek feedback, and understand their next steps, if we fail to do so ourselves? Our mantra is that teachers should never hold an instructional strategy in higher esteem than their students' learning. And what we mean by that is that our collective efforts should be aimed at students' learning, which allows them to make changes in real time to ensure that this happens. Of course, this begs the question, what is *Visible Learning* and what evidence do we have that this is the right focus for schools, teachers, and students?

QUESTIONS FOR REFLECTION

As you review the list of characteristics of visible learners, think about your current or past students. Can you identify any visible learners?

What Is Visible Learning?

In reality, *Visible Learning* describes a constellation of efforts. It is a research database, a school improvement initiative, as well as a call to action to focus on what works best to impact learning. The *Visible Learning* database is comprised of over 1400 meta-analyses, with over 70,000 studies and 300 million students. That is big data when it comes to education. In fact, some have said that it is the largest educational research database amassed to date. To make sense of so much data, John focused his work on meta-analyses.

A meta-analysis is a statistical tool for combining findings from different studies with the goal of identifying patterns that can inform practice. In other words, they are studies of studies. The tool that is used to aggregate the information is an effect size. An effect size is the magnitude, or size, of a given effect. To draw an imperfect but functional comparison, consider what you know about how earthquakes are measured. They are reported on an order of magnitude, called a Richter scale. Some earthquakes are imperceptible except through specialized measurement tools. Other earthquakes have a minimal "shake" that results in small, momentary impact, but with no lasting effects. A fewer number register high on the Richter scale and have a definitive impact on the area. Effect size information, like the Richter scale, helps us understand the impact of an educational influence in more measurable terms.

For example, imagine a study that demonstrated statistically significant findings ($p < 0.01$ for example) for having students stand while learning math. People might buy stock in "standing tables" and a new teaching fad would be born. But then suppose, upon deeper reading, you learned that the standing students had a 0.02 month gain over the control group, an effect size pretty close to zero. You realize that the sample size was so large that the results were statistically significant, even if the size of the learning gain is not very meaningful. Would you still buy standing desks and demand that students stand while learning math? Probably not (and we made this example up, anyway).

Understanding the effect size lets us know how powerful a given influence is in changing achievement—in other words, the impact for the effort. Some things are hard to implement and have very little impact. Other things are easy to implement and still have limited impact. We search for things that have a greater impact, some of which will be harder to implement and some of which will be easier to put into play. When you're deciding what to implement to positively impact students' learning, wouldn't you like to know what the effect size is going forward? Then you can decide if it's worth the effort. John was able to

Teachers should never hold an instructional strategy in higher esteem than their students' learning.

demonstrate that influences, strategies, actions, and so on with an effect size greater than 0.40 allow students to learn at an appropriate rate, meaning at least a year of growth for a year in school. (We need to be careful, however, as this .40 is an average across students from ages 4 to 20, across subjects, across countries.) While it provides an overall average, often specific conditions can be more critical—such as whether you are measuring a narrow construct (like vocabulary words known) compared to a wider construct, such as creative thinking). Before this level was established, teachers and researchers did not have a way to determine an acceptable threshold and thus weak practices, often supported with studies that were statistically significant, continued.

Let's take two real examples. First, let's consider individualized instruction. There have been many efforts to provide individualized learning opportunities for students. To help people understand effect sizes, John created a barometer so that information could be presented visually. The barometer for individualized learning can be found in Figure Intro.1. As you can see, the effect size is 0.23, well below the zone of desired effects of 0.40. This is based on 9 meta-analyses with 600 studies. There is some surface logic to individualized instruction, but it seems that effective teachers are able to engage larger groups of students in meaningful learning. Moreover, on many occasions students learn from other students and such interaction, as we will see, can be powerful. Great teachers know the similarities among their students and then allow for their differences.

QUESTIONS
FOR
REFLECTION

How would you explain effect size as it relates to student learning?

Second, let's consider feedback. Effective feedback is timely, specific, and includes actions that students can take to further their learning. As can be seen in the barometer in Figure Intro.2, the effect size of feedback is 0.73, well above the threshold of 0.40. This is based on 23 meta-analyses with 1,287 studies. It seems reasonable, then, to focus on the quality of feedback over individualized instruction for students. It needs to be noted that the effect of feedback is relatively high but we also point out that the effects of feedback can be remarkably variable; and this variability needs to be understood (see Clarke & Hattie, forthcoming).

Figure Intro.1   Effect Size of Individualized Instruction

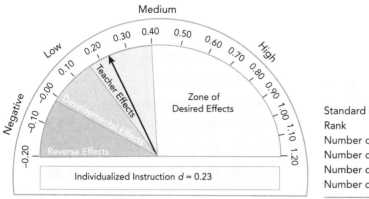

KEY	
Standard error	0.056 (Medium)
Rank	100th
Number of meta-analyses	9
Number of studies	600
Number of effects	1,146
Number of people (2)	9,380

Source: Hattie, J. (2009). *Visible learning: A synthesis of over 800 meta-analyses relating to achievement.* New York, NY: Routledge.

Figure Intro.2   Effect Size of Feedback

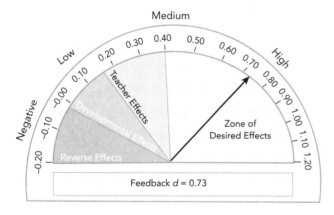

KEY	
Standard error	0.061 (Medium)
Rank	10th
Number of meta-analyses	23
Number of studies	1,287
Number of effects	2,050
Number of people (10)	67,931

Source: Hattie, J. (2009). *Visible learning: A synthesis of over 800 meta-analyses relating to achievement.* New York, NY: Routledge.

And that's the power of the *Visible Learning* database in creating school change. When a school focuses on what works best, more students learn more. Having said that, the database is huge and can be overwhelming. The second generation of *Visible Learning* work has centered on taking specific influences and translating them into classroom practice. For example, Donohoo (2017) focused her efforts on collective teacher efficacy, a powerful influence on student learning. We have previously focused on the use of Visible Learning in literacy (Fisher, Frey, & Hattie, 2016), mathematics (Hattie, Fisher, Frey, Gojak, Moore, & Mellman,

2017), and science (Almarode, Fisher, Frey, & Hattie, 2018). This current work attempts to focus on increasing students' responsibility for their own learning as yet another way to marshal the Visible Learning knowledge base and make it come alive in the classroom.

Conclusion

We have a goal for schools and that is to make learning visible to every student. That's a tall order. It requires that teachers focus more on learning and less on teaching. Yes, we all use a range of instructional approaches, but is instruction resulting in learning? That means we have to know the impact we have on learning; we measure it and monitor it.

In order to make learning visible, we must create assessment-capable learners. Too many students are adult-dependent learners. Others are compliant learners. Neither will serve our society well. What we need are learners who understand their current performance, recognize the gap between their current performance and the expected performance, and select strategies to close that gap. When schools are filled with students who have those characteristics, learning becomes not only visible, but also palpable.

DEFINING ASSESSMENT–CAPABLE VISIBLE LEARNERS
and the Teachers Who Create Them

Meet Jose. It doesn't really matter what grade he is in or where he goes to school. What does matter is that he had a history of struggle in school and, in fact, was recommended by his previous school for grade-level retention. Jose's mom knew that simply retaining him and forcing him to repeat the same class with the same content was not the answer for her son. She transferred him to a different school, one that was focused on students assuming responsibility for their learning.

Two years later and Jose is performing nearly at grade level. He is also a lot happier and is much more engaged with his peers. The difference? Jose is becoming an assessment-capable visible learner. The idea is appealing, isn't it? Who wouldn't want assessment-capable visible learners? On the surface, that sounds like students who perform well in school. That is important; schools should be all about learning. But we mean much more by the phrase *assessment-capable visible learners*.

On a daily basis, Jose can tell you what he is supposed to be learning and he can tell you where he is in the overall learning progression. He understands that there is no "bad" place to be, and that he is focused on closing the gap between what he needs to learn and what he currently understands. Jose can say to himself "I know where I'm going," which is one of the signature characteristics of an assessment-capable visible learner. Perhaps more importantly, he knows what to do next to further his learning. In doing so, his attention is focused on learning and he is motivated to close the gap that he recognizes in his own current understanding. The tasks his teacher assigns provide Jose an opportunity to engage in learning that is just the right amount of challenging—not too hard and not too boring.

Jose also can select the tools he needs for the journey. For example, while working on an essay, Jose recalled prior lessons that focused on writing introductions. He chose an introduction type to match his topic. On another day, Jose asked for peer feedback on his draft, as he knows this type of support provides another learning opportunity. Jose's teachers have equipped him with cognitive and metacognitive tools, but it is up to Jose to select from the tools he has and then apply them to the learning task at hand. He also has come to understand *what to do when he doesn't know what to do*. That sounds complex, and it is. When Jose gets stuck, he has strategies in place to help him get unstuck. For example, when confronted with a complex mathematical task, Jose was not sure where to start. Rather than be stymied by this, he decided to reread the problem and identify the given and the units. He then asked himself what the problem was asking and check with a peer to validate his thinking. Jose struggled with this task, but he knows that he has to take action to figure out things even when he's not sure what to do.

He also engages in self-talk, in his head, reminding himself that he can be successful in the face of setbacks or when his learning progress stalls. He reminds himself that there is a wide range of supports available to him—teacher and peers—to ensure he is successful. In other words, he is beginning to see that his errors are opportunities for learning. This is key, as students often wrongly believe that errors are evidence of their character, rather than an expected and welcome part of learning. In Jose's school, teachers regularly comment, "*We celebrate errors because they're opportunities to learn.*" They teach their students how to recognize their own errors. Then these teachers leverage these errors for the learner's benefit.

Further, Jose knows that he has to track his own progress. Of course, his teachers also monitor his progress through formative evaluation of his work and summative tasks that allow him to demonstrate mastery. But Jose is an assessment-capable visible learner who knows that it is his responsibility to monitor his own learning. He doesn't only rely on his teacher to tell him when he has learned something. Jose does not wait for feedback from others; rather, he regularly seeks out feedback from his peers and his teacher.

In addition, Jose has been taught a number of strategies to use in self-assessment. For example, his teachers have provided students with a checklist for assessing their own participation within the group. Jose uses the checklist (see Figure 1.1) to monitor his engagement with peers

Figure 1.1　Self-Assessment for Collaborative Learning

During my collaborative group time, did I

☐ Track the speaker?

☐ Recognize and build on the comments of others?

☐ Remain focused on the topic at hand?

☐ Bring the group back to the task when we got distracted?

☐ Listen carefully to ideas I did not agree with?

☐ Seek consensus to help the group make decisions?

☐ Monitor my nonverbal behavior to ensure that it communicated that I was interested?

☐ Contribute to the group such that our tasks were completed?

online resources　Available for download at **resources.corwin.com/assessment-capable** during collaborative learning. But he doesn't do this simply to comply, which is the lowest rung of the learning ladder. Jose has come to appreciate that the quality of his engagement with peers has a direct effect on his own learning. His teachers have taught him that his learning is enhanced when he is an active participant in the discussion. He has discovered that he is particularly good at getting his group back on track when they lose focus. He also has learned a number of other ways to assess his own performance, including rubrics that he develops on topics that are of interest to him.

And finally, Jose recognizes his learning and teaches others. As he monitors his success, he notes where those successes lie, as well as which areas still require attention. He communicates this with his teacher (and others, including his family members) as he works to interpret data about his learning and set goals for mastery. He knows that learning is important and he is motivated by the success he experiences. This success drives him to want to learn more and the cycle starts again. Once he has attained the success criteria for the lessons, Jose looks for the next gap in his learning, comparing his current performance to the learning progression.

In order to build assessment-capable visible learners, you need your own success criteria. You need a vision of an assessment-capable visible learner.

For many people, this sounds idealistic and unattainable. But it did happen. It happened for Jose, a real student in a real school, with real teachers who understood the value of creating assessment-capable visible learners. Those teachers provided Jose and his peers with specific experiences that built their competence and confidence, which in turn reinforced the necessary characteristics that assessment-capable visible learners possess. It's not pie in the sky, but rather an attainable goal when school teams focus on a few things that work really well. To our thinking, assessment-capable visible learners, not just their teachers, think about their learning in complex and interrelated ways. And in order to build assessment-capable visible learners, you need your own success criteria. You need a vision of an assessment-capable visible learner. That's why we introduced you to Jose.

If there is one core message in this book that we want you to come away with, it is this: *Assessment-capable visible learners are cultivated by assessment-capable teachers.* They understand that learning is accelerated when three conditions are present: *skill, will,* and *thrill* (Hattie & Donoghue, 2016). Learners need to be equipped with the skills and knowledge, but also with the will to learn—this is the motivational component. When you combine skill and will, the result is the thrill of learning. It's the disposition that drives learners to investigate, explore, and take academic risks. Standing next to every assessment-capable visible learner is a teacher who is determined to foster these beliefs, dispositions, and abilities in every student. This teacher understands that her fundamental mission isn't teaching math, or reading, or science, or any other subject. Job number one is ensuring that her *students know how to learn.*

What Does It Mean to Learn?

A common dictionary definition of learning suggests that it is the acquisition of knowledge and skills through experience, study, or by being taught. That seems simple enough on the surface, but anyone who has tried to measure learning knows that the process is much more complex. To some, learning is memorization and recall. In fact, at some points in the history of education, students were expected to memorize texts and recite them. When they did so, their teachers indicated that they had successfully learned the content. Others suggest that learning requires demonstration and application. At other points in the history of education, students' performance on summative assessments was used as the sole measure of whether or not they had learned something. Many parents continue to subscribe to this type of learning and schools and districts around the country are often graded on student performance on these types of tasks.

More recently, some standardized assessments have been redesigned to measure deeper levels of knowledge, focused on students' ability to apply concepts, skills, and strategies in unfamiliar situations and to continue to acquire information and ideas on their own as evidence of learning. We believe that students, teachers, and families should value memorization and recall of the content information *if* it then leads to reducing students' working memory demand so that they go on to understand conceptual relationships, extend their ideas, and think critically. Memorization and recall have their place in the cycle of learning but rarely at the start and certainly not as an end of learning.

Standing next to every assessment-capable learner is a teacher who is determined to foster these beliefs, dispositions, and abilities in every student. This teacher understands that her fundamental mission isn't teaching a subject. Job number one is ensuring that her *students know how to learn.*

QUESTIONS FOR REFLECTION

In what ways do you currently measure and monitor student learning?

How do you support your students' ability to measure and monitor learning?

Consistent with learning theorists (e.g., Biggs, 1999; Bransford, Brown, & Cocking, 2000; Marton & Säljö, 1976), we have proposed that learning occurs across three phases—surface, deep, and transfer—and that there are specific strategies that align with each of these phases of learning (Fisher, Frey, & Hattie, 2016). Importantly, surface learning is not superficial learning. Surface learning focuses on one idea at a time, whether concept or skill. For example, when students are first introduced to the skill of making inferences while reading, they are performing at the surface level. They are learning what an inference is and are provided examples, often through modeling, as they examine examples and non-examples. They learn about the ways in which authors imply things so that inferences can be made.

At the deep level, students see connections, relationships, and schema between ideas and learn to organize skills and concepts. Deep learning often involves interacting with peers and provides students with "aha" moments as they discover these connections. The student who is learning to infer progresses to deep learning when she is able to explain and justify her inferences to others and when she sees the relationship between making inferences, predictions, activating background knowledge, recognizing vocabulary and word choice, and critical reading. It's this integration of ideas that signals the deep phase of learning.

When this student begins to apply knowledge in increasingly new and novel situations, the transfer level of learning is reached. For the student working on inferences, when she develops the habit of using this process while reading across text types and genres, applying her knowledge to increasingly complex texts and does this with automaticity, we would say that transfer has occurred. To our thinking, transfer is the goal of learning. When students reach the point of transfer, they own the concept or skill and know how to use it.

At the surface and deep levels, there are two processes that must occur to ensure that students have a chance to develop the transfer level of learning: *acquisition* and *consolidation*. As Hattie and Donoghue (2016) note,

> During the acquisition phase, information from a teacher or instructional materials is attended to by the students and this is taken into short-term memory. During the consolidation phase, a learner then needs to actively process and rehearse the material as this increases the likelihood of moving that knowledge to longer-term memory. (p. 3)

To ensure that students become assessment capable, teachers must actively help students learn how to learn, in part by helping them select appropriate learning tools (strategies).

Figure 1.2   **Aligning Instructional Strategies With Phases of Learning**

	Surface	**Deep**	**Transfer**
Acquisition	Note-taking	Concept mapping	Classification charts
	Annotations	Metacognitive strategies	Sorting, matching, and categorizing
	Summarizing	Elaboration and organization	Student-generated classification patterns
	Mnemonics	Strategy monitoring	
	Notebook reviews		Similarities and differences
Consolidation	Practice testing	Peer response groups and seeking peer support	Extended writing instruction (improve and elaborate on ideas, strive for cohesion, think aloud about process)
	Deliberate practice	Classroom discussions	
	Spaced practice	Student tournaments	
	Rehearsal	Self-questioning	
	Help seeking	Self-monitoring	
	Receiving feedback	Collaborative learning	

A list of common instructional strategies useful for each phase of learning is presented in Figure 1.2. As you consider these instructional approaches, it's important to remember the focus of this book: assessment-capable visible learners. If we are to be successful, students must learn to select from a range of strategies to move their learning forward. Teachers can organize learning experiences for students, but to ensure that students become assessment capable, teachers must actively help students learn how to learn, in part by helping them select appropriate learning tools (strategies). Students who are assessment capable are able to move through the surface, deep, and transfer phases of learning more adeptly. This is the catalyst—the fuel—needed to accelerate learning.

QUESTIONS FOR REFLECTION

Think about a time you have experienced deep learning.

What was it like?

How did you know you had learned?

What Fuels Learning?

Astute educators know that all that is taught is not necessarily learned. Our quest, then, is to determine what ingredients are vital for learning to occur. We ask ourselves, "What is the right combination of experiences that ensure learning? What conditions must be present? Should more time be spent on direct instruction or on dialogic instruction?" (e.g., Munter, Stein, & Smith, 2015). Debates rage in education about which strategies are most effective, and the ultimate answer lies in knowing your impact on your learners (Hattie, 2012). The strategies we teach our students to learn encompass four general categories (e.g., Boekaerts, 1997; Dingath, Buetter, & Langfeldt, 2008).

Four General Categories of Learning Strategies

- **Cognitive strategies** such as summarizing or estimating, especially when used to deepen understanding of the content being studied

- **Metacognitive strategies** such as planning, monitoring, and regulating the learning process

- **Motivational strategies** such as self-efficacy and self-regulation to remain focused and engaged in learning

- **Management strategies** such as finding, navigating, and evaluating resources and information

Assessment-capable teachers mediate the thinking of their students as often as they possibly can, so that their students can gain more insight into how and when they learn, and associate their actions to results.

Teachers whose mission it is to cultivate assessment-capable visible learners teach all four of these kinds of strategies and create opportunities for students to use them. They hold a metaphorical mirror up to students to promote reflection, self-questioning, problem solving, and decision making. Assessment-capable teachers mediate the thinking of their students as often as they possibly can so that their students can gain more insight into how and when they learn, and associate their actions to results. And they possess a clear vision of the kind of learner they are building because they know the characteristics of an assessment-capable visible learner.

Characteristics of Assessment-Capable Visible Learners

We have described a student, Jose, and noted why we believe that he is an example of one who is on his way to becoming assessment-capable. In doing so, we draw on the work of Absolum, Flockton, Hattie, Hipkins, and Reid (2009) in our thinking about increasing the role that students play in becoming assessment capable. We have organized the research evidence and our experiences into five factors that comprise the characteristics of assessment-capable visible learners, including the following:

- **I know where I'm going**. Students understand their current performance and how it relates to the learning intention and success criteria.

- **I have the tools for the journey**. Students understand that they can select from a range of strategies to move their learning forward, especially when progress is interrupted.

- **I monitor my progress**. Students seek and respond to feedback from others, including peers and teachers, as they assess their own performance. Students know that making mistakes is expected in learning and indicates an opportunity for further learning.

- **I recognize when I'm ready for what's next**. Students interpret their data in light of the learning intention and success criteria of the lessons as well as the overall learning progression to identify when they are ready to move on.

- **I know what to do next**. Knowing what to do *when you do not know what to do* is surely the mark of the educated person. It is the difference between knowing how to persist and simply giving up when faced with an early challenge. It is the essence of being a lifelong learner, one who knows how to research, organize information, and continue his or her own learning.

Video 1.1
Teaching Strategies for Visible Learners, K–5

resources.corwin.com/ assessment-capable

To read a QR code, you must have a smartphone or tablet with a camera. We recommend that you download a QR code reader app that is made specifically for your phone or tablet brand.

Helping students become assessment-capable is part of a larger initiative known as *Visible Learning* (e.g., Hattie, 2009), detailed in the Introduction. Reconsider the experiences we conveyed about Jose and see how many of his learner characteristics are consistent with those of a visible learner. Jose, like a growing number of students around the world, is surrounded by teachers who leverage high-yield influences to cultivate these characteristics.

Video 1.2
Teaching Strategies for Visible Learners, 6–12

resources.corwin.com/ assessment-capable

High-Yield Influences to Build Assessment-Capable Visible Learners

Next to every assessment-capable learner is a teacher who uses strategies and techniques to help the student take ownership of learning. These documented influences impact a student's ability to learn how to learn (Hattie, 2009). High-yield influences that point to the construction of assessment-capable visible learners include teacher clarity, expectations, challenge, self-reported grades, feedback, and agency and ownership for learning through goal setting. Mobilizing several high-yield influences at once further amplifies their power.

Teacher Clarity

As with the conceptual framework of assessment-capable visible learners, teacher clarity is really a constellation of ideas. With an effect size of 0.75 (with the potential for accelerating growth in one school year) it's worthy of attention. In essence, teacher clarity requires that the teacher knows what students need to learn, communicates those expectations to students, conveys the success criteria for students, and presents lessons in a coherent way. Teacher clarity is an important driver to improve student learning. Assessment-capable learners attend to the learning intentions and success criteria as a means to map their future learning. We will revisit teacher clarity in more detail in Chapter 3.

Teacher Expectations

All teachers have expectations for their students. Therefore, there really is no point in asking the question "Do teachers have expectations for their students?" The better question is "Do they have false and misleading expectations that lead to decrements in learning or learning gains—and for which students?" (Hattie, 2009, p. 121). The impact that teachers' expectations have on student learning is 0.43. Let's state it another way: If teachers expect their students to learn a full year (or more) of content for a year of input, they probably will. These expectations are communicated every day, from demeanor to the challenge of tasks. Expectations need to be at the forefront as teachers plan units of study and engage students in quality learning experiences.

Challenge

As we noted in the introduction, challenge is an important aspect of learning. Overall, challenging tasks have an effect size of 0.57. But when teachers ensure that students have a "Goldilocks" challenge, not too hard and not too boring, the effect size increases to 0.72. Students expect that school will be challenging, but not to the point of frustration and utter defeat. They also hope that they are not bored with tasks that seem meaningless and can be easily completed without much thought. Becoming assessment capable means helping students feel capable in the face of appropriate challenge. A misinterpretation of Dweck's (2007) work on growth mindset is that it exists as a state of being. It isn't used when the task is an easy one. Challenge is a necessary condition for growth mindset. Further, growth mindset isn't simply a rallying cry like

The Little Engine That Could ("I think I can, I think I can . . ."). Rather, it is a coping strategy that an assessment-capable learner can deploy when faced with a slog. In those situations, learners pause, take a deep breath, and then begin to consider what to do next when they don't know what to do. What does this mean for teachers? It means we must regularly create tasks that challenge students, equip them with problem-solving strategies, and assist them in making decisions about what they might do next. Under those conditions, a growth mindset can be developed.

Self-Reported Grades

In order for students to understand where they're going, they need to have an accurate sense of where they currently stand. With an effect size of 1.44, self-reported grades are a powerful way to strengthen student learning because it gives them the opportunity to take a measure of their current status. The evidence clearly suggests that students are acutely aware of their performance and understand their achievement levels. But if they have to rely on their teacher (and their grades) to tell them where they are and when they have learned something, they become dependent on adults, and they don't develop that internal compass they need to drive their own learning. Teachers of assessment-capable visible learners create opportunities for their students to understand their own current level of understanding and recognize when they don't know something. First grader Andrew told his mom that he would "meet the standard" on his math assessment several nights before it was administered, which he did. He knew what he knew and accurately predicted his success.

In order for students to understand where they're going, they need to have an accurate sense of where they currently stand.

Student Expectations of Their Learning

Schools that focus on developing assessment-capable visible learners encourage students to reach beyond their current expectations. With an effect size of 1.44, student expectations of self are a powerful driver of learning. These students receive consistent messages about mastery of learning (e.g., "I want to learn how to improve my use of perspective in my paintings"). Mastery of learning is an important belief for students (and their parents) to develop. Without intending to, schools sometimes reinforce some students' beliefs about goal setting for performance only (e.g., "I want to get a passing grade in art."). Students who only attend to performance often limit their expectations of themselves, determined to play it safe rather than engage in the kind of academic risk taking that learning requires. We betray the message about the necessity of errors in learning when we react to the mistakes of children as evidence of deficient character or ability. "Struggling" is situational, not identity. There is a monumental difference between saying "I'm stuck" versus "I'm stupid." Too often, children receive the unintended message that if you don't get it right the first time, you failed. In fact, if you routinely get everything right on the first attempt, it is an indication that there isn't a sufficient level of challenge for you. This is equally damaging for students who excel. Children and families who are focused only on performance ("straight As") reinforce a belief that playing it safe and limiting challenge is their key to success. Assessment-capable visible learners are resilient ones who rise to a challenge and are willing to go higher.

Agency and Ownership for Learning Through Goal Setting

When teachers and students have goals for learning, the impact is positive with an effect size of 0.56. This does not mean that teachers simply say "do your best" or that the goals focus on completing tasks, as was the case when a teacher said, "Our goal today is to finish the questions at the end of the chapter." Rather, goals should be focused on learning, not just doing. When school is reduced to an endless series of tasks to be completed, learning suffers immeasurably, as goals are reduced to a series of items to cross off on a to-do list. When students share a commitment to the challenging learning goals they (and their teachers) set, those goals are more likely to be attained. Fourth grader Melissa set a goal for herself, which was to "figure out how to add and subtract fractions with different numerators," and then set about trying to learn that, noting her mistakes and successes along the way.

Goals should be focused on learning, not just doing. When school is reduced to an endless series of tasks to be completed, learning suffers immeasurably, as goals are reduced to a series of items to cross off on a to-do list.

Essentially, the research on goal setting suggests that students live up to the expectations they, and others, have for them (Martin, 2013). Students set themselves expectations about what and how they can achieve and by age 8, these are pretty accurate. But our job is to mess them up and help students rise *above* the expectations they set for themselves. We can say to them, "What do you think you will receive for this assignment? A grade of B? Well, I can help you attain an A." The problem with too many expectations is that it sets a limit on the sense of satisfaction a student can obtain.

Feedback

We all want to know how we're doing, especially when we're trying to master a new concept or skill. But how that feedback is provided can either make us defensive and destroy the learning situation or propel us to new levels of understanding. Many of the other influences in *Visible Learning* also include feedback; it permeates the educational landscape. With an effect size of 0.73, it's something to value, especially when done well. At its core, feedback is "just-in-time, just-for-me information delivered when and where it can do the most good" (Brookhart, 2008, p. 1). Feedback is not limited to teachers giving it to students. Feedback sources also include self and peers.

What are some of the methods you use to manage agency, ownership, expectations, and goal setting within your classroom?

What are some methods you would like to implement?

We'll return to a more detailed discussion of feedback in Chapter 5 of this book but it's important to recognize that, first and foremost, teachers have to see student work and performance as feedback to themselves. That makes some people uncomfortable, but as John (Hattie, 2009) noted, "feedback to teachers helps make learning visible" (p. 173). Seeing student learning as feedback to oneself as a teacher opens the door to all kinds of other feedback. In this way, feedback becomes a "consequence of performance" (p. 174) and thus is seen as a natural set of actions following the completion of some effort.

Teachers of assessment-capable visible learners use high-yield influences to foster their students' ability to learn how to learn. Importantly, they have a vision of what an assessment-capable learner looks and sounds like, and they search relentlessly for evidence of student growth. They reflect on their own impact, understanding that student learning is feedback about their teaching. They adjust accordingly to strengthen their students' skill, will, and thrill. In the chapters that follow, we delve more deeply into the ways in which educators can help students become assessment-capable visible learners.

First and foremost, teachers have to see student work and performance as feedback to themselves. That makes some people uncomfortable, but as John noted, "feedback to teachers helps make learning visible" (p. 173).

Conclusion

To accomplish the goal of making learning visible, educators first need to know what works best, and when those things work. Simply said, some things are much more likely to ensure learning than others. Focusing on actions that are most likely to ensure learning is sensible and can prevent a lot of problems later (see Hattie, 2009, 2012, for a list of evidence-based approaches). Having said that, it's important to remember that strategies cannot be used in the generic. Rather, teachers should carefully consider the phase of students' learning needs and which approaches are more likely to guide thinking.

When students are assessment capable, and when all of us know our impact, we set the conditions for transfer to occur. As a result of transfer, teachers do not have to spend time at the start of every year providing students review and reteaching of previous content. Instead, learning is extended beyond expectations and young people are future-proof. In other words, they know how to learn, which equips them to be able to learn about concepts and skills we haven't even dreamed of yet. They are ready for anything that the world hands them and they know how to succeed.

It is important to note that this learning is always about "something," hence the content of the curriculum is critical. While we do not cite the actual knowledge or specific understanding that is the focus of learning, we need to be mindful of the moral claims we make when we choose this content. The reason for developing assessment-capable visible learners is for them to know, and care about, important knowledge. Thinking is a means to this knowledge end, and knowledge is the building block for further learning.

In the chapters that follow, we will leverage these principles to articulate a coherent set of instructional practices and introduce you to educators who foster assessment capability in their students. Together, the teacher and these assessment-capable visible learners possess the following abilities:

- Know their current level of understanding (Chapter 2)

- Understand where they're going and have the confidence to take on the challenge (Chapter 3)

- Select tools to guide their learning (Chapter 4)

- Seek feedback and recognize that errors are opportunities to learn (Chapter 5)

- Monitor progress and adjust their learning (Chapter 6)

- Recognize their learning and teach others (Chapter 7)

ASSESSMENT–CAPABLE VISIBLE LEARNERS...
Know Their Current Level of Understanding

Maria Gomez and Jessica Avalos are comparing their spelling tests. They are in third grade and their teacher, Marcelo Contreras, uses a differentiated approach for his students to learn to spell words. The students completed an assessment at the beginning of the year which estimated their developmental spelling skills and identified word patterns they still needed to learn. This served as a starting place for students to further develop their spelling prowess.

Maria is on lesson 14, which focuses on *r*-controlled vowels and there are 18 words on her list including *stork*, *storm*, *market*, *partner*, and *artist*. Jessica is on lesson 9, which focuses on words with /ou/ sounds including *clown*, *round*, *power*, *thousand*, and *mountain*. Each day during the week, students quiz each other on their word list. For each lesson, Mr. Contreras has the words on slips of paper so that the words can be shuffled. Each day, the practice quiz occurs in a random order. The daily spelling quiz allows students to assess their developing understanding and focus on the words that they really need to learn (Templeton, 2003). The students self-check their spelling after the quiz, circling right on the word any place where a letter is missing, a letter was incorrectly added, or if letters were transposed. They also grade themselves on each spelling word, not the whole list, so that they can monitor which words they have mastered. (They give themselves an A if the word is spelled correctly, a B if there is one error in the word, and a C if the word contains two errors.) Mr. Contreras knows that students can read words to their partners that they may not be able to spell on their own.

> Teachers should work to develop a learning climate where progress, not status, is celebrated.

Listening to Maria and Jessica highlights the first characteristic of assessment-capable visible learners. They recognize which words they have mastered and which words they still need to learn. They also know that there is no bad place to be in terms of current learning, and that everyone is focused on getting better. Mr. Contreras works to develop a learning climate where progress, not status, is celebrated. As part of their conversation, Maria asks her partner which words she spelled correctly. This leads to a discussion about patterns and areas to study. Here's part of their conversation:

> **Jessica:** *I got 11 of them right. That's way better than yesterday when I just got 6. I got all of the* ou *ones right, plus* clown, *but I already knew that word because I really like clowns and my dad takes me to see them.*
>
> **Maria:** *You did really good. That's a lot for one day. Where did you get the other ones wrong?*
>
> **Jessica:** *In most of them, I put* ou *and not* ow. *I have to study and learn the ones with the* ow *because they sound like the* ou *words that*

I have been learning. Plus I missed coward. *That's a bonus word, but I want to get it right. See, I spelled it* couword. *So I got a C on that word but I got a B on all of the other words.*

Maria: *That's good, right? You have 11 As, 6 Bs, and 1 C. What's your goal for tomorrow?*

Jessica: *I think that I will get 17 right. I might not yet get* coward *right, but I'll try. I have to practice the* ow *words with my mom so that I can get out of Lesson 9.*

Maria: *Now let's talk about mine. It's not so good. I only got 2 As but that's really not fair because I already know* horse *and* March. *So really, I didn't get any better from yesterday. I think that I need to practice these more. When we're done with writing workshop, can you practice these with me again? I don't want to wait until tomorrow.*

This example came from a third-grade classroom and it focused on spelling, but from our perspective, all students should understand their current level of performance, or current level of understanding, for anything that their teachers teach or that they want to learn. Assessment-capable visible learning starts with an understanding of what you already know. It's important for students to recognize that they already know a lot and that learning is not starting from scratch for every lesson. Assessment-capable visible learners also need to revise their thinking about their current level of understanding as the lesson progresses. They need to recognize that they are learning and that what they have mastered is important. In doing so, students are motivated to continue to expend the effort required to learn. The starting point for students to know their current level of performance is in the development of confidence in their teacher. When students have confidence in their teacher, they trust that it is acceptable to not know some things and that their teacher is dedicated to closing the gap between what they already know and what they need or want to know.

QUESTIONS FOR REFLECTION

What are some ways your students could monitor their progress and mastery in your class?

Confidence in the Teacher

Learning is a risk-taking endeavor. It requires that the learner put her faith in the teacher's ability to lead. The credibility of the teacher inspires confidence and a willingness to be open to risk. It is also a source of motivation for the student to draw on when the learning is difficult or when a setback occurs. Being able to tell herself, "I know my teacher knows what he's doing, so I'll be okay" speaks to the trust she has in her teacher.

Teacher credibility involves three constructs: "competence, character (or trustworthiness), and perceived caring" (Finn et al., 2009, p. 519). The first, competence, is related to the teacher's projected subject matter knowledge and ability to organize instruction. (Nancy recalls her six-year-old granddaughter's assessment of a substitute teacher's first day: "Nana, she doesn't know the right math!") The second construct, which is character, includes perceptions of fairness and respect. (John recalls one of his sons saying that a teacher "treated everyone the same." When asked how, John's son said, "It's not like we all get the same rewards or punishments regardless of what we do; there is no fairness in that.") The third, which is caring, is understood by students to include responsiveness and nonverbal actions such as eye contact, smiling, and open and inviting body language. Maria and Jessica have confidence in Mr. Contreras because he has earned a reputation with them of being knowledgeable, organized, fair, and optimistic about his students' learning. (On the other hand, Doug recalls a professor of his who said, "I don't know how you're going to learn this, but it's on the midterm.")

Middle school English teacher Soraya Garcia-Estrada actively works at building her credibility with her students. "I work with homeless children, and gaining their trust can be challenging," she said. Ms. Garcia-Estrada exhibits all the expected behaviors of a caring teacher: greeting students and their families at the door, kneeling down at eye level when talking privately to a child, and interacting with them in affectionate ways. But the teacher understands that if she is going to ask her students to take academic risks, she needs to do more than make them safe and comfortable.

Ms. Garcia-Estrada says, "I will often tell my sixth graders 'we're going to do something that only eighth graders usually get to do' or remind them about the gains they've made this year already." When meeting with Rodrigo, a student not yet achieving at expected levels, Ms. Garcia-Estrada began by reviewing his reading scores. *"Let's look for the big jumps you've already made. I see one right here. Between December and February, you moved up two levels in reading. That's something to celebrate!"* The teacher then asks Rodrigo what he did to be so successful. Rodrigo replies that he was starting to read aloud to his baby sister, but that lately he hadn't been able to because of other family circumstances.

"I can see why that would help," said the teacher. *"Why don't we do that right here at school? I'll ask our first-grade teacher if she has a student who could be a reading buddy for you to tutor. Would you be willing to do that? I would love to recommend you for this important job."* The boy smiles and nods yes. In the span of a short conversation, she had built trust, expressed optimism, and displayed immediate responsiveness. But she also got Rodrigo to consider his own learning and what might help him become a more successful reader in the future. By adding this element, Ms. Garcia-Estrada helped this student become more confident in himself as a learner.

When students have confidence in their teachers, they are ready to learn about what they don't know. In other words, they are ready to confront the limitations of their current levels of understanding. Without confidence in the teacher, students often misbehave rather than ask for help or let others know that they don't understand. As Randy, a ninth grader, once said to a teacher he came to trust,

> *In middle school, I would rather be bad than stupid. I knew when I didn't understand something, but when that happened, I caused problems because I didn't want anyone else to know, even the teachers because I didn't think they cared about me. Here, in this class, it's okay for me to tell people that I don't understand because you always say "there's no bad place to be as long as you are learning." And it's true in here. Everyone is at a different place and we're all learning. So, I can tell the truth about and ask for help when there are things that are confusing to me.*

Yes, recognizing when you don't know something is an important part of becoming an assessment-capable visible learner. As Randy noted, he knew his current level of performance in middle school but was unwilling to share it with others because he did not trust the adults in his learning environment. However, his confidence in his teacher and in the psychological safety of his ninth-grade classroom enabled him to open himself up to learning. He was able to drop some of his defensive stance, setting the stage for reflecting on his learning, rather than perceived character flaws.

Recognizing When You Don't Know Something

Jessica, one of the students in the opening scenario, was able to articulate what she didn't know about her spelling words. Randy indicated that he often knew what he didn't know, although he was unwilling

> When students have confidence in their teachers, they are ready to learn about what they don't know. Without confidence in the teacher, students often misbehave rather than ask for help or let others know that they don't understand.

to share it with others. A further challenge is that some learners don't know what they don't know. Posing challenges and questions are useful for causing students to consider an idea they had not previously considered. The ability to recognize when you don't know something is an element of metacognition, which is thinking about one's own thinking (Flavell, 1985). The ability to think metacognitively helps us make decisions about our own learning, and learners who are metacognitively aware are accurately able to articulate their own strengths and plan for the use of strategies.

But metacognition is not unilaterally present. Its relative presence or absence is influenced by the learner's knowledge and can in fact be discipline-specific (Zohar & David, 2009). Metacognition includes knowledge of strategies (which we will discuss further in Chapter 4) as well as knowledge of the task (Zohar & David, 2009). When learners don't know much about the task at hand, they need guidance in delineating what the learning task is going to involve. As we will note in the next chapter, learning intentions and success criteria can accomplish this. The ability to perceive the difficulty of a task is necessary in order to choose the steps required to be successful. It also prevents overestimation of one's ability to complete a task, a phenomenon that can occur when a learner has low ability but is not able to recognize her own lack of skill (Kruger & Dunning, 1999). This bias toward one's own skill level expresses itself in daily life, too. In one study of U.S. drivers, 93% of those surveyed gauged their own skills in the top 50% of all drivers (Svenson, 1981).

> Asking students about their estimations of task difficulty both before and after assignments can foster their ability to more accurately calibrate their internal gauge.

Asking students about their estimations of task difficulty both before and after assignments can foster their ability to more accurately calibrate their internal gauge. Tenth-grade teacher Felipe Sanchez provides such opportunities for his students on math tasks. When assigning work, he asks students to review the task and answer three questions in writing about the assignment:

- What will be the easiest part of this assignment?

- What will be the most difficult?

- How much time do I expect it will take me?

"After they've finished the task, I ask them to respond again to these three questions, this time after the fact," said Mr. Sanchez. "I want to build their ability to estimate what it will take to finish it, and then to compare their predictions to their conclusions and results."

For the students focused on spelling, each had an opportunity to consider what they knew and did not yet know. Further, they had a clear sense of what the task would entail and they had engaged in this task many times. Maria and Jessica were able to make generalizations about their learning and draw conclusions about what they needed to focus on next.

Metacognitive Awareness

Metacognition, defined as thinking about one's own thinking, includes recognizing when one doesn't know something. The ability to be aware of what one doesn't know is mediated by age, and younger children have a more limited capacity to do so than older ones. But "limited" doesn't mean "not at all." Instructional routines that prompt self-questioning assist young children in noticing what they do and do not know. Importantly, instructional routines can move students forward in planning what they need to know next in order to answer their questions.

Diana Mendoza uses a See-Think-Wonder language chart to promote metacognitive thinking in her kindergarten students (Ritchhart, Church, & Morrison, 2011). After reading *Houses and Homes* (Morris, 1995), Ms. Mendoza turned her students' attention back to the photographs in the book, featuring homes throughout the world. The students were particularly intrigued with the image of houseboats at the foot of the Himalaya Mountains in India. Sensing their interest, she used this tool (which the children had used many times before) to foster their metacognitive thinking, especially to recognize their own knowledge (see Figure 2.1).

She asks them first just to report on what they see in the photograph by looking carefully at each quadrant. Ms. Mendoza records their thoughts in the first column as children describe the mountains in the upper two quadrants of the photograph, and the water and a houseboat transporting sand in the lower half. Next, she asks her students about their thinking as they examine the photograph. *"I think the people use their boats to work and live because there is a bedroom and there are people buying things"* offers Oliver. *"Can you give me an example of other places where people would both live and work at the same place?"* the teacher asks.

QUESTIONS FOR REFLECTION

How does metacognitive thinking apply to your content area?

How do students "think about their thinking" as readers, scientists, mathematicians, historians, or artists?

Figure 2.1   See-Think-Wonder Language Chart

See What do I see? What is my evidence?	Think What do I think about what I see? What are my examples?	Wonder What do I wonder about what I see? What are my questions?

Source: Adapted from Ritchhart, R., Church, M., & Morrison, K. (2011). *Making thinking visible: How to promote engagement, understanding, and independence for all learners.* San Francisco, CA: Jossey-Bass.

online
resources ⬙   Available for download at **resources.corwin.com/assessment-capable**

Oliver thinks for a minute and then says, *"Well, my grandpa has a camper [recreational vehicle/caravan] and he has all his stuff in it. He lives in for the weekend when he comes to visit and he does his carving in there, too."* Other students add that it might be like if a police officer lived in her cruiser or an airplane pilot lived on board. *"Now that's a really interesting idea,"* Ms. Mendoza says. *"Oliver's example of his grandfather is a bit like the people in this photo because their house moves, too. But it is different because they are using it for work. The police officer and the pilot use their vehicles for work, but it would be hard for them to live in them, too."* Freddy giggles. *"Where would they put the kitchen?"*

After writing their partial examples in the second column, she moves on to the third. *"This seems really unique. We haven't thought of any examples that are just the same. So what questions do you have now? What would you ask these people if you could?"* Now the questions come quickly, and she lists them on the language chart:

- How much room do you have for sleeping and cooking?

- Where do the children go to play?

- How old do you have to be to drive the boat?

- The mountains look cold. Is the water cold?

- Do you have a pet?

Ms. Mendoza looks at their chart of questions and says, *"You've come up with some great topics that we don't know yet. How could we find out some of these answers?"* With help from their teacher, the students add that they can read about life in the region, and one student speculates that *"we could search for a video on YouTube 'cause they probably have that there, too."* Later, their teacher remarks, "Developmentally, these metacognitive habits are still a few years away. But habits are built through practice. I'm always impressed with how insightful they are. They just need outlets to express it. And most of all, I want them to appreciate that not knowing something is a chance to wonder and investigate."

Assessing in Advance of Instruction

One pitfall in getting comfortable with a grade level or discipline is the risk that you've seen it all before. After all, a decade of teaching the same age group can lull one into a false sense of security about students' prior knowledge. Prior knowledge is a strong predictor of future performance, less so in the primary grades, but growing in significance throughout high school (Hattie & Donoghue, 2016). But each cohort of students has its own idiosyncratic knowledge base, and one sixth grader isn't representative of every sixth grader. What does come with experience is the ability to make more precise predictions about likely misconceptions students possess and the ability to think like a novice. Common misconceptions abound and astute teachers know how to directly address them. The relative inability to predict misconceptions and understand how novices approach new concepts is referred to as the *expert blind spot* (Nathan & Petrosino, 2003). The researchers found that inexperienced secondary mathematics teachers had difficulty in translating what they knew as experts into sequential steps that would be understood by math novices (i.e., their students). Nathan and Petrosino's (2003) findings, by the way, have been replicated in studies involving other disciplines and grade levels. Some of this comes from experience, but that will only take you so far. Assessing what students know in advance of instruction will throw light on the gap between where they are and where you want them to go.

Cloze Assessments

There are a number of techniques teachers can use to assess students' prior knowledge. One technique is a cloze assessment (Taylor, 1953). Cloze assessments use a 250-word passage that captures the major concepts for a unit of study that has yet to be taught. Every fifth word from the passage is deleted, leaving the first and last sentences intact. Students fill in the missing words (make sure they understand that this isn't a test, but rather an assessment you are doing to make instructional decisions), and score accordingly:

- 60% correct or above indicates the student possesses a strong knowledge base about the topic

- 40% to 59% correct indicates they have some background knowledge and are ready for future instruction

- 39% correct or below indicates the student might have gaps in background knowledge that need to be addressed

The numbers may seem artificially low, but keep in mind that you are not supplying them with a word bank, and that some of the incorrect responses will involve substitutions that do not change meaning (e.g., *a* for *one*). The length of the passage or the rate of deletions may be adjusted, based on students' age or language proficiency. For example, second-grade teacher Angelica Norris constructed a shorter passage and deleted every seventh word for her students before teaching a social studies unit about maps (see Figure 2.2). The underlined words are those that will be deleted on the student version. "I wrote a passage of 116 words that captured some of the important concepts I will be teaching toward for the map unit I'll begin next week," Ms. Norris explained. "I take out every seventh word so they can use more contextual clues, but I don't give them a word bank. The bonus is that I can also see if there's anyone who's making syntactical errors, since those tell me something about their grammatical knowledge of the language."

Her purpose for assessment isn't only for measurement—it also serves as an advance organizer for their learning. "I describe these cloze assessments as 'learning maps,'" Ms. Mendoza said. "It's a guide for their future learning." In order to do so, the teacher recognizes that the information can't remain only with her. "If I was the only one who kept the results, it would limit the insight that my students can gain from recognizing what they do and do not know," she said. "I give this back to them, and from time to time throughout the unit, we return to this early assessment. We discuss how our growing knowledge helps us to better complete this learning map."

Figure 2.2   Cloze Passage for Second-Grade Social Studies

Maps help us find our way. <u>A</u> map is an illustration of a <u>community</u>.
It can show roads and buildings. <u>Maps</u> can show the land, such as
<u>mountains</u>, rivers, and fields. Some maps are <u>printed</u> on paper. Other
maps are digital, <u>like</u> those on phones and computers. All <u>maps</u>
have labels so you know the <u>names</u> of places. All maps show you
<u>the</u> direction. Directions on a map are <u>north</u>, east, south, and west.
A compass <u>rose</u> helps you find the direction. All <u>maps</u> have a way to
measure the <u>distance</u>. This measurement is called a scale. <u>We</u> use maps
to walk, to drive, <u>and</u> to plan trips. Without maps, we would get
lost a lot!

online
resources   Available for download at **resources.corwin.com/assessment-capable**

Self-Assessment

Assessments in advance of instruction can activate background knowledge, an important factor in knowing what you know and don't know about a topic, and help students identify what they already understand. Seventh-grade humanities teacher Keith O'Neill has his students self-assess their own knowledge and experiences in advance of a unit on the history of the theater (see Figure 2.3). "I like these self-assessments because it gives me an idea of what their experiences have been. But even better, it gets them thinking about what they've done and sort of forgot about," he said. "What I really like is when I hear one of my students whispering under his breath as he's taking this, saying, 'Oh yeah, I did do that!'"

However, these assessment approaches have diminished impact if students are not included in reviewing the results. It really is surprising how often students take assessments only to see scores, rather than afforded the chance to analyze their performance. Students own their data, not teachers. The third graders in the scenario at the beginning of the chapter were encouraged to analyze their performance so they could make plans for their future learning. Without opportunities to do this kind of analytical thinking, students have a much harder time recognizing what they don't know. Another method for determining the prior knowledge of students while alerting them to what they do not yet know is to prepare a short quiz for students to complete. For example, students can take a brief preassessment quiz on upcoming content and

Figure 2.3   Theater Self-Assessment

We will be studying the history of the theater in different societies and cultures.
Please take a few minutes to tell me about your knowledge and experiences with theater.
Place a checkmark in the box that best describes you.

	I have seen one on TV or at the movies.	I have seen a live production.	I have been in a production.	This will be a new experience for me.
A musical play				
A modern play				
A play by Shakespeare				
An ancient Greek play				
An opera				

online resources   Available for download at **resources.corwin.com/assessment-capable**

score their responses in order to alert them to what they know and don't know about the next unit of study.

Another method is to provide students with a partially completed concept map illustrating the conceptual relationships of future content. Students can revisit these maps and add more details during the unit, thereby witnessing their own developing learning. Similarly, students can list the vocabulary they initially associate with a new topic of study using an ABC chart. As a preassessment in advance of a unit on bats, the second graders in Liz Herman's class listed terms such as *flying*, *wings*, and *vampire*. After two lessons on the topic, the children independently added additional terms, such as *mammal*, *fruit*, and *insects*. At the end of the weeklong unit, students returned to their ABC charts and were invited to add new terms. Ms. Herman now saw occurrences of words like *nocturnal*, *roost*, and *colony*. "I like using the ABC charts because they get to see their own growth as they add new words," she said. "I'm not giving them the words to copy. They are determining which words to add, although I give them assistance with spelling," said the teacher.

Ms. Herman explained that she challenges her students to use as many of the terms as they can in their summary writing. "By doing a written summary before, during, and at the end of the unit, they get to see how their knowledge has grown."

Self-Ranking

Most curriculum materials include a list of major outcomes or objectives for the unit of study. But how often do we share those with our students? Use these lists with students in advance of instruction by inviting them to rank the objectives according to perceived difficulty. Washington state fifth-grade teacher Karin Janssen uses state curriculum unit outlines for students to rank order the standards associated with each unit. Before a unit titled "The Legacy for Us Today," Ms. Janssen shared the grade-level expectations and asked each student to rank them according to perceived difficulty:

- I understand that significant historical events in the United States have implications for current decisions and influence the future.

- I can evaluate how a public issue is related to constitutional rights and the common good.

- I understand that civic participation involves being informed about how public issues are related to rights and responsibilities.

- I can research multiple perspectives to take a position on a public or historical issue in a paper or presentation.

- I can evaluate the relevance of facts used in forming a position on an issue or event.

- I can engage others in discussions that attempt to clarify and address multiple viewpoints on public issues based on key ideals.

- I can prepare a list of resources, including the title, author, and type of source, date published, and publisher for each source, and arrange the sources alphabetically.

"I change these into 'I can' statements and review them with the class, then have them put them in rank order from most difficult to least difficult using the survey tool in our school's learning management system," she explained. "I get the results, which help me to target instruction and supports, and differentiate a bit more precisely," Ms. Janssen said. "But it also has a great effect on students, too. They are actively thinking about their current knowledge and skills and making a plan for where they will need to devote more time and effort," she said. "I also have them revisit their rankings as we get nearer to the end of the unit so they can decide how accurate they have been in predicting their current status and what it took to be successful."

How Sure Are You?

Most of us have used K-W-L charts to encourage students to consider what they know about a subject, what they want to know, and later, what they have learned (Ogle, 1986). Many of us have also had individual students insist that they know something that is actually quite inaccurate. (Nancy recalls one of her fourth graders confidently stating that the pilgrims who landed in Plymouth Colony in 1620 discovered America, and that's why we celebrate Thanksgiving.) The temptation to abandon the K-W-L and immediately begin teaching is hard to resist.

However, one method for addressing this is to ask students to brainstorm what they believe they know about an upcoming topic of study, and then to write each statement on a sticky, one idea per note. The students then affix each of their stickies to a number line chart extending from Uncertain to Possible to Certain. This invites students to engage in some speculation, while leaving room for uncertainty. Students who possess inaccurate information might at least acquire a bit of doubt due to the initial discussions with peers during this activity. The students in Matt Baker's earth science class did this when they studied ocean currents. Some of them noted that circulation clockwise in the Northern Hemisphere and counterclockwise in the Southern Hemisphere, and they were pretty sure about it. Others noted that the wind caused the currents but were not very sure about that idea. Still others said that the currents change with the phases of the moon but were very unsure about that.

Anchoring

Once teachers have a sense of what students already know, they can use that to their advantage to anchor new knowledge to existing knowledge. Anchoring fosters schema as students begin to make connections and see relationships among concepts. These cognitive moves are crucial for moving from surface levels of learning to deeper learning, and further enhance a student's application and extension abilities. One method for doing so involves using a concept map known as an anchoring table to link established learning to new learning (Bulgren, Schumaker, & Deshler, 1997). Figure 2.4 shows an example of the completed work developed by a middle school science class studying the vascular system. The teacher began her lesson with a review of

Video 2.1
Helping Students Notice What They Do and Do Not Know

resources.corwin.com/ assessment-capable

Getting students to think, and to notice their own thinking, is vital if students are going to gain a sense of where they're going.

previously known understanding, in this case a unit from earlier in the year on river systems (seen in the left column). She then followed by teaching about the new information on the vascular system (seen in the right column).

The power of anchoring tables lies in the center column, as students and the teacher engage in extended discussion about the shared characteristics of the other two. Finally, they co-construct and write a definition or description of the new concept at the bottom of the chart. The usefulness of this approach is in the shared development of these concepts. Although the end product may be just a few sentences, it represents extended discussion. Students don't become assessment-capable learners by copying what their teachers have already written. That's hands on but minds off. Getting students to think, and to notice their own thinking, is vital if students are going to gain a sense of where they're going.

Figure 2.4 Anchoring Table

Known Concept: River Systems	Shared Characteristics	New Concept: Vascular System
Water moves through a system of rivers that flow in one direction.	Fluids in both systems flow in one direction only.	Blood moves through the vascular system and flows in one direction.
River systems are connected to smaller tributaries, streams, and small creeks.	These systems are a network of large vessels that connect to smaller ones.	The circulatory system is a network of connected blood vessels that can be large, and capillaries, which are smaller.
Water in the river system carries oxygen, carbon dioxide, and other chemicals and nutrients that other living organisms depend on.	Fluids transport vital gases and nutrients that maintain health.	Blood carries oxygen, carbon dioxide, hormones, nutrients, and amino acids. Other body organs depend on these to function.
A blockage in a river system, such as a dam, will cause water to back up and overflow its banks.	Blockages can be harmful to these systems.	A blockage in the vascular system will cause blood to back up. Blood vessels can burst if the overflow is too great.

My Understanding of the New Concept:

The vascular system has characteristics in common with river systems. The vascular system is a network of blood vessels that carry gases and nutrients to other organ systems. Harm to these systems can result when a blockage occurs.

online resources 🔍 Available for download at **resources.corwin.com/assessment-capable**

Conclusion

It's not enough for teachers to know their students' current performance levels. Students must understand, and use, this information as well. Having said that, we don't want to minimize the value of teachers knowing their students' current performance levels. Understanding this information allows teachers to plan lessons and differentiate their instruction. Without clear knowledge of students' prior knowledge and skill development, teachers run the risk of wasting a lot of time teaching things that students already know and can do. Armed with good information about students' current performance levels, teachers can establish appropriate learning intentions and success criteria, which are the focus of the next chapter.

In addition to understanding their current level of understanding, assessment-capable visible learners have to be comfortable sharing where they are in a learning progression with others, including their peers and their teachers. When their teachers foster habits of seeking out and knowing one's current status and future direction, students can ultimately answer these questions: *Where am I now? Where am I going?* In doing so, students assume increased responsibility for their learning and become their own teachers, which is the ultimate goal of schooling. Our hopes are not that we create adult-dependent learners, but rather independent learners who continue to seek out information, generate ideas, and influence the world around them. Knowing your current performance level is the first step to realizing the goal of creating assessment-capable visible learners.

ASSESSMENT–CAPABLE VISIBLE LEARNERS...

Understand Where
They're Going and
Have the Confidence to
Take on the Challenge

© Elizabeth Crews/PhotoEdit

Courage

"Whoa. Mind blown."

Those might not be the words you expect to hear from an assessment-capable visible learner, but Lucas really is one. He's a tenth-grade student enrolled in an anatomy and physiology course, part of a Career and Technical Education (CTE) pathway at his high school. His CTE teacher, Gretchen Harrison, has been leading a unit on the nervous system, and the day's lesson is on language centers in the brain's cerebral cortex. She had stated her learning intentions at the beginning of class, pointing out specific locations that would be the focus of the lesson. She gestures to a diagram of the brain in the students' materials: *"Your purpose today is to understand the functions of Wernicke's area and Broca's area on speech and language, and relate them to specific aphasias."* Ms. Harrison further explained the success criteria, which further guides their learning: *"Based on your understanding of the anatomical features of these two areas, you will explain the physiological results when either is damaged."* She continues, *"This is something that at first is going to seem a bit challenging. But I've also witnessed your growing expertise about the nervous system. You've got the tools to accomplish this."* The teacher then asked her students to take a few minutes to answer the first two of three metacognitive questions they use when embarking on new content learning. These will be the basis for an exit slip they will submit at the end of class (see Figure 3.1):

1. *What?*

2. *So what?*

3. *What's next?*

Lucas began by writing some notes to himself to address the first question. He considered what he already knew about these language areas and their locations (*Broca's is in the frontal lobe, and Wernicke's is where the parietal and temporal lobes meet*) as well as what he doesn't know (*I don't know what the effects of damage would be*). He then addressed the second question, which causes him to consider the relevance of the topic: *So what about this? People use language to communicate. If there's damage, it must really impact a person's life because maybe they can't communicate any more.* During the next hour, Lucas and his classmates work with their teacher developing notes about the neuroanatomy of both areas, and they speculate about how a language disorder, or aphasia, might manifest itself. *"I need to think about what I already know to solve this,"* Lucas reminds himself. *"There's a logical pattern here. I just need to find it."* He and his table group soon arrive at consensus, agreeing that since Broca's area is in the motor region of the frontal lobe, damage must impact speech production. Only after the groups have engaged in this deductive reasoning does Ms. Harrison show time-lapsed video clips of a teenager who suffered a stroke that damaged her Broca's area, tracing her progress over the next several years as she slowly recovered. It was at this point that Lucas said, *"Whoa. Mind blown."* When asked why, he said, *"Two reasons. First, it's amazing to see her speaking change over the seven years after her stroke. But I also have to say that using what we knew about brain function helped our group to nail it. Pretty proud of that."*

Figure 3.1   **Ms. Harrison's Reflective Student Questions**

1. **What?** Take a few moments to write down what you already know about this topic. Based on your prior knowledge, what are your predictions? Next, write one or two statements or questions you have about today's topic. What don't you know but hope to learn?

2. **So what?** Relevance is important in learning. Based on what you know and what you hope to learn, in what ways might this affect other body systems?

3. **What's next?** Reflect on today's learning, and its implications for future learning. What do you anticipate you will learn about soon? Your ability to predict future concepts based on present knowledge is a good indicator of your learning.

 Available for download at **resources.corwin.com/assessment-capable**

Near the end of the lesson, Ms. Harrison asked students to write their explanation and rationale for Broca's aphasia and Wernicke's aphasia, followed by their third question: *What's next?* The purpose of this question is for students to anticipate what information they will need to deepen their knowledge. Sometimes it is crafted in the form of a statement, but more often it is posed as a question. Lucas wrote the following: *Broca's aphasia makes it hard for the patient to produce sentences more than a few words long. But what gets damaged if they aren't producing any speech at all? It can't be the same area of the brain. I think this is what we'll learn next.*

How could you use Ms. Harrison's reflective questions—*What? So what? What's next?*—to foster assessment-capable learners?

So why is Lucas an assessment-capable visible learner?

- He bears the hallmarks of a student who understands his current level of performance relative to the stated learning intentions and success criteria.

- He used the opportunity his teacher provided to examine his own current state of knowledge, and identified what he did and didn't know yet. Recognizing what one doesn't know is an early key to learning because in doing so, one becomes actively enlisted in the learning, not merely a passive receiver of knowledge.

- He displayed some of the self-regulation needed, such as persisting in looking for logical patterns, having confidence that he could do so, and considering what might come next in the learning sequence.

- Lucas, his teacher would tell you, is not afraid of challenge. He exhibits an inquiring and speculative persona that signals a level of motivation.

- Finally, he is able to maintain a level of attention to the topic of study, thereby reducing the likelihood that he will miss essential concepts.

Now consider what the teacher has done, as she is an important part of the equation. She communicates clear learning intentions and success criteria, both of which contribute to teacher clarity. Ms. Harrison creates opportunities for her students to actively consider what they already know, which builds the learner's habit to preassess. Her instruction links new knowledge to prior knowledge, thus more firmly anchoring skills and concepts. She actively seeks to build relevance to further engage her students and conveys a level of credibility that inspires confidence in her students. She also expresses a confidence in their ability to learn and grounds that in what they have accomplished previously, nurturing a growth mindset. Effective teachers guide the learning journey, which means the teacher must have the destination in mind. This requires more than being able to mouth the standards. Effective teachers are able to articulate coherent learning intentions and success criteria. After all, if the teacher can't define the targets for learning success, what hope could there possibly be that a student would be able to define them?

Video 3.1
Creating Learning Intentions and Success Criteria, Part 1

resources.corwin.com/ assessment-capable

Learning Intentions and Success Criteria

At the heart of what teachers accomplish (or not) are the goals set for students. There is much talk about having high expectations for students.

This goes well beyond the state, territory, or province standards that guide schools. While standards document the stated learning goals, the true influencers are the teacher and the learner. The standards themselves are not sufficiently detailed for creating the manageable progressions that lead the learner. These daily steps come in the form of the learning intentions the teacher lays out for students. There are several reasons why these work so well. First, stated learning intentions have a priming effect on learners. They signal to the student what the purpose is for learning and prevent students from having to fall back to the lowest rung on the ladder, which is compliance. A second reason why learning intentions are so effective is that they cause students to see the relationship between the tasks they are completing and the purpose for learning. Students need to understand that a particular math activity is for the purpose of building conceptual understanding, or that the assigned reading is to build the background knowledge they'll need for the lab experiment they'll soon be completing.

Success criteria let students in on the secret that has been too often kept from them—what the destination looks like. Imagine getting into an airplane that was being flown by a pilot who didn't know where she was headed. Rather, a control tower would contact her at some unspecified time in the future to let her know she had arrived, or worse, that she missed the mark entirely. That is a completely irrational way to fly a plane. Yet students often have a similar experience. They're flying their own learning plane but have little sense of where they are headed. Wouldn't the trip be completed more successfully and efficiently if the pilot knew from the beginning where she was going? Now imagine how much more successful and efficient learning would be if we enlisted students in their learning journeys! Success criteria signal the learner about the destination and provide a map for how they will get there. Further, these criteria empower learners to assess their own progress and not to be overly dependent on an outside agent (their teacher) to notice when they have arrived. That does not mean that the teacher is unimportant, or that teachers do not need to evaluate students' learning. Like a control tower, you are providing corrective feedback, giving data the pilot can use, and advising her about when and where to proceed. But the important point here is that the pilot and the control tower coordinate their work. One without the other would be unthinkable.

The evidence on the effectiveness of learning intentions and success criteria is impressive. Hattie and Donoghue (2016) examined 31 meta-analyses of more than 3,300 studies related to success criteria and reported an overall effect size of 0.54. Embedded within these are effects on the learner, especially in causing students to plan and predict, set goals, and acquire a stronger sense of how to judge their own progress. Instructional

Learning intentions have a priming effect on learners. They signal to the student what the purpose is for learning and prevent students from having to fall back to the lowest rung on the ladder, which is compliance.

Video 3.2
Creating Learning Intentions and Success Criteria, Part 2

resources.corwin.com/ assessment-capable

strategies that further learners' ability to do so include co-construction of concept maps, providing advanced organizers, and utilizing worked examples to further understanding of what success looks like. Procedures such as these allow discussion and negotiation about what actually constitutes mastery, rather than leaving such understanding to chance.

It is crucial to note that while we name learning intentions and success criteria as two separate components, in practice, they are coupled. The learning intentions speak first to the teacher's ability to plan instruction such that the outcomes for a unit are segmented into a clear and coherent set of lessons that build student knowledge, skills, and conceptual understanding. Learning intentions are expressed as statements that signal to students *what* they will be learning, *why* they are learning it, and *how* they will know they are successful. These learning intentions can be expressed as the purpose for learning, which includes sharing the content, language, and social objectives for the lesson (Fisher & Frey, 2011). Fourth-grade teacher Matt Pappert uses learning intentions and success criteria with each lesson in a science unit about endangered species of plants and animals that are native to the region. His students have been investigating assigned species and will be constructing infographics to share with the class. Mr. Pappert posts his purpose so that his students can refer to it throughout the lesson. It reads

> *Learning intentions are expressed as statements that signal to students* what *they will be learning,* why *they are learning it, and* how *they will know they are successful.*

- *Content purpose:* Identify and understand reasons that species are endangered and actions that can be taken to protect a given species.

- *Language purpose:* Describe, with evidence, the visual features and textual content contained in a persuasive message.

- *Social purpose:* Engage in active and careful listening as a reviewer and as a presenter.

In addition, he tells his students,

> You've been working on your projects all week, and today we're going to use some peer critiques so you can get some feedback in order to revise. This is an important step for developing your infographic. The information needs to be accurate before you can begin designing the visuals. We've looked at quite a few, and as a class you came up with a quality checklist for elements of a good infographic. So this morning you will self-assess for accuracy and completeness. You'll need feedback from someone else to do that, so our language purpose today is to present the information you've gathered to a partner, using the peer critique process

we've been using this year. That means that your social purpose is also important, and it's all about careful listening. When your partner is presenting to you, listen without interruption and take notes so you can repeat what you think you've heard and ask any clarifying questions. When you're getting feedback from your partner, listen carefully to what he or she has included or left out, and think about his or her questions thoughtfully.

As Mr. Pappert's students move to meet with their peer critique partners, the teacher checks in with specific students so he can gain feedback about how well the learning intentions and success criteria are understood. Jamison and Hailey are able to explain the purpose in their own words to the teacher's satisfaction, but Edward has more difficulty. Mr. Pappert spends a few minutes with Edward, and they revisit the infographics checklist developed earlier in the week. As teacher and student work together, Mr. Pappert realizes that although he set the learning intentions, he could have further strengthened the link to the success criteria. In response, he regains the attention of the whole class, and reviews the checklist with them. *"I realized that I failed to use one of our tools when I was explaining the purpose,"* he said. *"Let's take a minute or two to look at the checklist. That's our success criteria, and it's something you and your partner should use during your peer critiques."* Later, Mr. Pappert said, "When someone doesn't fully grasp what they're doing, that's feedback to me about my teaching. You can't allow your ego to get in the way of their learning. If someone doesn't get it, that's on me."

Video 3.3
Learning Intentions and Success Criteria in High School Math

resources.corwin.com/ assessment-capable

"I can . . ." Statements

Teachers can use "I can . . ." statements to organize their success criteria. They can also use checklists, language charts, and a variety of other tools to ensure that students understand what learning looks like. "I can" statements have been used in elementary schools fairly widely as a way to provide student-friendly language. But their use is not limited to young children. In a chemistry class at the start of the school year, the teacher identified two success criteria for an in-class activity:

- I can describe how subatomic particles affect mass, atomic number, and charge.

- I can calculate the number of neutrons, protons, and electrons in an isotope.

These two success criteria are foundational to understanding and using the periodic table and will serve as the basis for much of the learning students with do in the class. If students do not master these, the teacher will know that she has to change the lesson or her strategies. Assessment-capable visible learners track their progress on success criteria, monitor their success against those criteria, seek feedback and assistance when they struggle, and recognize when they have learned something. Much rests on the quality of the success criteria.

Relevance

We can't leave the subject of learning intentions and success criteria before addressing the issue of relevancy in learning. Learning intentions and success criteria address the acquisition and consolidation of skills and concepts; relevancy addresses motivation to learn. All learners need to have some insight into why they are learning something. Some learning purposes come with relevancy baked into them, such as successfully completing a driver's education course in order to gain a permit or license. But the relevancy of much of the school-based knowledge we teach is not so readily apparent to the learner. It can be a struggle to frame the relevancy of content if one possesses a belief that everything needs to lead to a distant and aspirational ending, such as focusing on graduating from college when you're still in fourth grade. Quite frankly, a lot of what we teach doesn't really fit into the driver's license kind of scenario, and when it's too far in the distance, it's not very motivating anyway. Relevancy needs to be closer to home. Why are syllables important? *Because they help us read big words.* Why do we need to know the difference between a simile and a metaphor? *So we can use these techniques in our own writing to express ideas without being too obvious.* Why are we learning to balance equations in chemistry? *Because no substance on Earth can exist if it violates the Law of Conservation of Matter. And because balancing equations allows us to understand how food becomes fuel for our bodies and why soap removes grime, and lots of other things including some things you might want to invent on your own.* Taking the time to address relevancy not only fosters motivation, but it also deepens learning as students begin to make connections to larger concepts. In other words, an understanding of the relevancy of one's learning moves students forward from declarative (factual) knowledge, through procedural and conditional knowledge—from *what* to *how* to *when*.

There are at least three ways to make learning relevant. The first is that the information could be used outside the walls of the classroom. As we noted earlier, it can't be too far in the distance, but understanding that learning has utility beyond the confines of the four walls of a classroom can guide students' attention. When Marcus came to understand that writing introductions would be useful in other classes and in his letter applying for a job, he was much more interested in what his English teacher had to say.

Video 3.4
Communicating Relevance

resources.corwin.com/ assessment-capable

A second way to make learning relevant involves students learning about themselves as learners. And who doesn't love to learn about oneself? Some lessons help students think about their problem-solving skills and strategies. Others help them develop composing processes. And still others help them clarify which learning strategies are useful, productive, and fun. When Kira had the opportunity to learn about decision-making skills as part of a science lesson, she was all in. Her teacher made personal decision making valuable and important, and the students could not wait to get started.

A third way that teachers can make learning relevant is to note the value of the lesson in becoming an educated member of the community. For some students, this is a bit of a stretch but others enjoy knowing things that other people know. For example, when the students in Brad Maddox's fifth-grade class learned about the 1790 decision to move the capital of the United States from Philadelphia and instead to build a permanent capital city in the area we know as the District of Columbia, the teacher said,

> Some people know the history, but a lot of people don't. The politicians of the time wanted to appease Southern states that supported slavery. We've learned about other times when appeasement was used to calm down a group. They didn't want a Northern capital. I think that people who understand why the capital was moved understand political motivation, which can help them out when they want to negotiate. And I think it would be great to talk with your families about the reason that the capital moved. Let's see how many people we can educate!

QUESTIONS FOR REFLECTION

Consider the three ways that teachers can make learning relevant.

What are some ways you have made learning relevant?

What would you like to try?

Teacher Clarity

Establishing the learning intentions and success criteria aid assessment-capable visible learners in understanding where they are going in their learning. But these instructional moves on their own would be insufficient for learning. Students thrive when their teachers possess a level of clarity about how the instruction is organized and delivered. *Teacher clarity*, defined as "a measure of the clarity of communication between teachers and students—in both directions" (Fendick, 1990, p. 10) elegantly captures the reciprocity that is necessary for learning to occur. Both teacher and student are engaged in communication about the lesson and the learning that (should) accompany it. Hattie (2012) notes that teacher clarity exercises a strong influence on learning, with an effect size of 0.75. The four dimensions of teacher clarity outlined by Fendick (1990) are

1. **Clarity of organization** demonstrated through a logical sequencing of tasks that align with learning intentions and success criteria

2. **Clarity of explanation** signified by their cohesiveness and accuracy

3. **Clarity of examples and guided practice** that illustrate skills and concepts and move students toward increasing levels of independence

4. **Clarity of assessment of student learning** through frequent checks for understanding and formative evaluation that is responsive to learning needs

Video 3.5
Teacher Clarity

resources.corwin.com/
assessment-capable

We have addressed the first dimension of teacher clarity, and we will return to the importance of assessment in a later chapter. But we haven't touched on the need for explanations, examples, and guided practice. Keep in mind that teaching is not a one-way transmission model, where teachers try to fill the heads of students with bits o' facts. Assessment-capable visible learners are involved and actively engaged in their learning. They are not passive vessels waiting to be filled with heaps of knowledge. But that does not mean that the learner is cast adrift to find and use information, with little guidance from the teacher. Rather, sound instruction must possess a high degree of precision and should result in actions the learner can take up to keep the momentum going. Instruction should be crisp and clear, filled with examples that best illuminate the principles under investigation. Most of all, teachers should have a plan for how students are going to try out the ideas. Passive learners rarely have insight into what they know and don't know. Ask them if something makes sense, and if they have not yet tried it, they are likely to naïvely nod their heads in silent agreement. Students often don't know what they don't know until they try it for themselves. Clear explanations provide the foundation, but guided instruction gives them the scaffolded experiences they need when they first apply new knowledge.

Clear Explanations and Guided Instruction

Tenth-grade history teacher Courtney Soo needs to introduce her students to the information about the Battle of Stalingrad in their unit of study about World War II. She wants her students to recognize the significance of the five-month battle, both in terms of its scale and its significance in the war on the eastern front. She reviews the posted learning intentions and success criteria:

- *Content purpose*: Identify the major features of the Battle of Stalingrad and why it is called a turning point in the war.

- *Language purpose*: Use and interpret visual representations of quantitative data, including interactive maps.

- *Social purpose*: Work collaboratively with your group members, tracking the speaker and ensuring equity of voice.

"Here's how you will know you are successful today. You'll write a short constructed response at the end of the period, in which you explain why it was a turning point in the war," Ms. Soo explains. For the next 20 minutes, she provides a coherent lecture on the details of the battle, using multimedia supports to illustrate the advancement of the Germans on the Eastern Front in the spring and summer of 1942, before reaching Stalingrad. Using photographs, she illustrates how the weather changed from late summer to the deep Russian winter, capturing the plight of soldiers and civilians as circumstances became increasingly desperate. "Before I share some of the big numbers of this battle—casualties, munitions, territorial losses—I want you to work at your tables with the primary source materials I've given you."

Imagine what your classroom would look like and sound like if learning intentions and success criteria were laid out for students. Describe it.

Students open the folder to find World War II–era photos of German and Russian soldiers and generals, short passages taken from firsthand accounts of participants, and a structured note-taking guide. For the next fifteen minutes, students read about the background of the individual they will portray, and then share their passages with one another. A German soldier recounts his suffering as he systematically lost fingers due to frostbite. A Russian soldier relives his terror during hand-to-hand combat with the enemy. Other students at the table read battlefield orders from Hitler and Stalin, each forbidding their armies to withdraw. After their table readings of the primary source materials, the students discuss the psychological toll on both sides.

Ms. Soo doesn't see that as being the end of learning, however. She knows it is relatively easy to engage students in an empathic understanding of the events. But she also wants them to recognize the cost of the battle to the German and Russian military forces. She brings them back together to weave in more details. This time, they are viewing a variety of graphs that illustrate the civilian and military casualties, the loss of munitions, and most importantly, the halted advancement Germany had been making up until this point in the war. Once again, Ms. Soo has them explore a second set of primary sources, such as the German announcement made to the people about their army's defeat, the demoralized responses in the German media, and jubilant press clippings from Allied nations. *That's the first time they ever admitted they lost,*" said Simon, a student. "*That must have felt like a kick in the stomach because the German military was so sure they were going to win.*"

After listening to student-read passages about celebratory announcements around the world, Valerie, another student, remarked, "*You can really see how much respect the Russians got from other countries like the U.S. and Great Britain. Their status went way up.*" Near the end of the lesson, Ms. Soo has students write an exit slip in response to the questions posed through the content purpose. The students rated themselves, on a scale of 1 to 5, with 5 indicating that they had mastered the learning intention and 1 noting that they were totally lost. Ms. Soo reads exit slips to make some decisions about her next steps for instruction. "I'm looking to see if they know why it's called a turning point, both from a military standpoint and a psychological one. Wars are always about people, not machines, and I want them to see how tactics are affected by human emotions."

Student learning in Ms. Soo's class was amplified because of her careful attention to the way information was delivered. She is knowledgeable about her subject, to be sure. More importantly, she possesses a deep understanding of how it is that students learn and what effective instructional moves are needed to foster learning. She created collaborative learning opportunities for students, developed compelling materials to foster discussion, and posed questions that caused her students to

Knowing that someone is in charge, and is able to create a psychologically safe learning environment, makes one a bit more willing to take risks and accept challenges.

think critically. As noted before, a teacher's ability to present content in an organized fashion further impacts a learner's confidence, an important factor of teacher credibility. With an effect size of 0.90 (Hattie, 2012), teacher credibility exerts a powerful influence that doubles the speed of learning.

The teacher's clarity and credibility contribute positively to a student's willingness to take on a challenge. All of us encounter various learning challenges throughout our lives—in fact, without the stretch, learning would not occur. But knowing that someone is in charge, and is able to create a psychologically safe learning environment, makes one a bit more willing to take risks and accept challenges. Learners are an essential part of this equation. Their ability to direct their attention is critical, as is our ability as adults to cultivate their attention and leverage it for learning.

Attention in Learning

Attention is essential to memory. All learners use memory to encode, store, and retrieve knowledge. Attention and memory are essential for deepening knowledge, building schema, and transferring learning to new and novel situations (Schunk, 2012). But every learner's attention is finite. Younger students typically have a lesser ability to attend for long periods of time, compared with older students. Other factors influence one's ability to attend, including environmental conditions as well prior knowledge of and interest in the topic. Attention is critical for discerning similarities and differences, which is key to moving from declarative (factual) and procedural (process) knowledge to the conditional knowledge necessary for making decisions about when concepts and skills are best deployed.

As learning deepens and skills become increasingly fluent, learners need to expend less attention on some information and can instead attend to new knowledge. Reading is a case in point. Emergent readers use a great deal of their attentional resources to figuring out the code of written language and must devote a large portion of their cognitive capacity to figuring out the letters and letter combinations that make up words. But as they become more fluent decoders, they reduce the amount of attention they give to decoding and can increasingly pay more attention to comprehending the meaning of the text. In other words, when some things are "learned," working memory can be devoted to more complex thinking. This process, which LaBerge and Samuels (1974) called automaticity, is crucial for learning in any number of content areas, not just reading.

Attention is dually influenced, externally by the teacher and internally by the student. Sound practices for gaining and maintaining student attention include

- *Using clear and consistent signals* ("*Be sure to annotate your questions in the margin of the text.*")

- *Priming students for future learning* ("*Next we're going to look at four milestones in early human civilization.*")

Students can also self-regulate their attention, and their capacity to do so matures through growth and practice. Kindergarten teacher Laura Miller teaches her students such practices so that they can activate them as needed. "We start each day with some breathing and stretching exercises," she explained, "and we use these throughout the day." Ms. Miller reminds her students to check in with their own bodies and feelings. "I take photographs of the students in different poses, such as pretending they are a flower growing from seed to plant. They crouch down low to the ground and then slowly rise and spread their arms wide." At various points during a lesson, especially when she sees outward signs of loss of attention, she invites them to "*shake their wiggles out*" or "*take five belly breaths*" and links these movements to methods for refocusing their attention. She tells them, "*Sometimes I notice my attention wandering. That's when I use these same strategies so I can make sure I'm not missing anything!*"

But Ms. Miller also wants to move from co-regulation with the teacher to self-regulation by the students themselves. She confers regularly with them about reading, writing, and mathematics, and usually adds a question or two about their favorite ways to refocus their attention.

"Just yesterday Zach [a student] told me that his attention after lunch is hard. No surprise, right? But when I asked him what he did about it, he told me that his current favorite is using the marching exercise. When I asked him why, he told me it gets the blood back up into his brain so he can do math better! That's remarkable insight for a five-year-old." Ms. Miller knows that monitoring students' regulatory strategies is important for making decisions about when to fade scaffolded support in order to build independence.

Motivation in Learning

Motivation and interest further expand a student's ability to attend to their learning. Emotion plays an important role in motivation, so first and foremost is the consideration for, and development of, a positive learning climate. When students see their classroom as a place where mistakes are viewed as opportunities to learn, and learning is seen as a cause for celebration, motivation increases. Another important factor is creating conditions that allow students to become more autonomous in their own learning. And as students are successful in their learning, their motivation can increase. Student assessment learners gain much motivation from learning (and motivation does not always precede learning). Choice contributes to autonomy and creates positive emotions that fuel learning. However, choice is not the only path for fostering motivation. Challenge is another element that can be utilized to capitalize on motivation. And motivation contributes positively to learning, with an effect size of 0.48 (Hattie, 2009). One way to accomplish this is in linking success criteria to a variety of ways to demonstrate mastery of a topic.

Fifth-grade science teacher Aisha Taylor provides a range of ways her students can show their learning about electrical circuits, including building a simple circuit, drawing a diagram of one, or recording a video in which they explain the process. She asks them to choose a functional use for the circuit, such as powering a digital clock or light bulb. "This is foundational knowledge. I want them to be able to explain the flow of electrons. But it's also a stepping stone to even more choice. The next unit is robotics, and they'll need to use principles of circuitry to make their robots work."

Ms. Taylor is leveraging another element of motivation, which is interest in the topic. To be sure, some instructional units lend themselves to higher levels of student interest, like robotics in the elementary classroom. But other techniques are likely to tap into student interest, such as examining age-appropriate controversial topics. Eighth-grade English teacher Kendra Washington used bullying as a theme and gave students choice from a curated list of readings, including *Smile* (Telgemeier, 2010), *Wonder* (Palacio, 2012), and *Backlash* (Littman, 2016). "The topic resonates with middle schoolers, and giving them a choice of reading selection is motivating, too," she explained. Ms. Washington begins each semester with an online ballot for her students to vote on unit topics. "I've got more units than I have time to teach, so letting them choose the topics actually helps me a lot." In addition, she requires each of her students to propose and complete an investigation of a research topic every semester. "They propose, and I listen. I've had students choose everything from Laura wanting to learn about self-driving cars to Justin who wanted to develop tips for starting a modeling career. You can't fully anticipate what students' individual interests will be. But if we never ask, how will they possibly be cognizant of their own interests and the paths to get there?"

When students see their classroom as a place where mistakes are viewed as opportunities to learn, and learning is seen as a cause for celebration, motivation increases.

Aspiring to Challenge

Motivation is also sparked by the desire to achieve mastery of a challenging skill or concept. Watch an aspiring athlete practice for hours on layups in basketball or juggling and dribbling techniques in soccer, and you get the idea. In fact, learning can't occur in the absence of challenge—it's stagnation, not progression. Assessment-capable visible learners understand that challenge is necessary on the road to mastery and are resilient in the face of temporary setbacks. A growth mindset is critical for facing challenges without giving into defeat. But Dweck (2016) warns against the "false growth mindset" that communicates a misunderstanding about its variable nature. "No one has a growth mindset in everything all the time," says Dweck. "Everyone is a mixture of fixed and growth mindsets" (Gross-Loh, 2016; also Hattie, 2017).

Most important of all, a growth mindset isn't a state of being—it is a coping skill one chooses (or chooses not) to draw on in the face of challenge. And a growth mindset isn't necessary when engaged in an easy task because there is no need to cope with anything. A growth mindset is fostered in relation to challenge. Students who rarely confront a difficult task are robbed of the opportunity to cultivate a growth mindset. Instead, they are failure deficient.

One's mindset is influenced by one's previous experience with the skill or concept. Students who don't know much about a topic of study *and* are aware that they don't know enough yet have an opportunity to cultivate that growth mindset as a means to persevere in the face of an obstacle. But praising their effort while ignoring the failed attempt doesn't help students move toward mastery or to develop a growth mindset. Students need to be able to examine the strategies they used and formulate new plans to try out in the next attempt. One element necessary for doing so is to recognize when they don't know something.

Video 3.6
Developing
Academic Self Efficacy

resources.corwin.com/
assessment-capable

Self-Efficacy and Self-Regulation

Sixth grader Rodrigo's experience with his teacher, described in Chapter 2, contributed to his growing sense of self-efficacy, which included his belief that he is up to the task and possesses the skills and character to do so. Bandura (1997) introduced self-efficacy as a driving force in the learning process, noting that "self-belief does not necessarily ensure success, but self-disbelief assuredly spawns failure" (p. 77). Learners' self-efficacy contributes to their willingness to engage in academic risk taking, a necessary component in the learning equation. As with other constructs internal to the learner, self-efficacy is discipline specific. All of us have experienced rising and diminishing levels of self-efficacy as we traveled from mathematics class to English, from art class to physical education.

Academic self-efficacy is an important factor in self-regulation. Self-regulation involves a collection of behaviors and dispositions, including the ability to self-observe, self-judge, and self-react (Bong, 2013). The ability to self-regulate is mediated by a learner's developmental level and experiences. Students need to be consistently drenched in opportunities to notice their thinking and feelings, make judgments about their status, and act upon their conclusions in ways that are growth producing. Ms. Harrison's *What*, *So What*, and *What Now* questions are designed to prompt self-observation. Ms. Garcia-Estrada's question about Rodrigo's reading improvement caused him to self-evaluate. Ms. Miller's stretching and breathing exercises with her kindergartners are an example of strategies students can use in reaction to their self-appraisals. In addition to maintaining focus, students with strong self-regulatory behaviors choose more challenging tasks, are better at selecting strategies, put forth more effort, and display lower levels of anxiety (Pintrich & De Groot, 1990). Bandura and others (e.g., Caprara et al., 2008) noted that in an increasingly technology-driven world, one in which information is readily available in a few keystrokes, self-efficacy is more critical than ever because it contributes to flexibility of thought in swiftly changing environments.

> Self-regulation involves a collection of behaviors and dispositions, including the ability to self-observe, self-judge, and self-react.

Self-efficacy, unlike other constructs such as self-esteem and self-worth, is futures oriented (Bong, 2013). Self-esteem and self-worth are drawn from past experiences, but academic self-efficacy is predictive. A learner asks, "Given what I know and don't know, and given my resources and current status, how likely am I to be successful at this task?" Therefore, learners need a strong sense of what the performance expectations are, and where they currently are relative to mastery. Like other factors internal to assessment-capable learners, this ability is nurtured by caring adults at home and at school.

Conclusion

An assessment-capable visible learner possesses a level of attention and motivation that drives their learning. That attention focuses on a student's current performance level, the expected performance as expressed in a learning intention, and the success criteria that will be used to determine whether or not sufficient learning has occurred. Teachers and students have a role to play in helping students know where they are going in their learning journey. Of course, students don't all arrive in our classrooms fully actualized. Rather, their teachers build the cognitive and metacognitive habits that make it possible for them to make learning visible to themselves. No child is "unmotivated," but some may have not yet encountered the right formula for unlocking their motivation. In other words, they haven't met you. Assessment-capable learners need assessment-capable teachers.

ASSESSMENT–CAPABLE
VISIBLE LEARNERS...
Select Tools to
Guide Their Learning

Alisha has a dilemma on her hands, but she's not going to give up now. This sixth grader has been investigating animal rights as part of an interdisciplinary research report she is developing. Alisha and her team are going to produce a 60-second public service announcement on responsible pet ownership, advocating spaying or neutering of cats and dogs to curb the population of unwanted animals. They had selected this topic after considering and discarding other ideas for their community service project. Her dilemma at the moment is in figuring out how to organize the multitude of facts into a coherent and persuasive message.

Fortunately, her teacher Isla Gregory has established a system for students to receive feedback and support from her and one another. Stations around the room are labeled *Scripting*, *Video Production,* and *Editing*. Alisha considers each of these stations and decides that the script the team initially developed needs more revision, so she heads to the scripting support table. Once there, she finds several supports. There is a checklist for considering the audience and the overall message, which Alisha considers and discards. "We've already done that, and it hasn't changed since we got all these facts together about spaying and neutering," she thinks to herself.

Next, she looks at the templates Ms. Gregory has provided. One is a two-column template that matches the video shot list to the narration. "We're going to need this soon, but not yet. First we need to get our facts organized before we can write a script," she thinks silently. "I need something else." Alisha's face lights up as she examines a template for creating a storyboard. "This is what we need." The template includes space to sort and separate problems from goals, and facts from reasons (see Figure 4.1). Alisha chooses this template for her group to use next and uploads it digitally to their workspace. Ms. Gregory checks in briefly with Alisha about her decision and nods in approval. The teacher later explains,

> I don't want my students to remain overly dependent on procedures at the expense of recognizing their own choices. We've done some video production before, with lots more scaffolding. But if they're going to grow as strategic thinkers, I can't allow them to just follow along in a lockstep kind of way. Once they know the process, I need to step back a bit and give them room to plan and resolve problems.

These decisions are essential in the life of an assessment-capable visible learner. Alisha needs opportunities to consider which tools and strategies she will use and for what purpose. It is analogous to the range most of us have experienced with cooking. Some would-be chefs don't progress beyond close adherence to a recipe, never straying far from the

Figure 4.1   Video Planning Template

Purpose	Our Ideas	What could this look like visually? (Draw a picture.)
Problem: What is the problem you want to highlight?		
Message: What is the message you want your audience to understand?		
Action: What action do you want them to take?		
Facts: What facts do you have that will persuade them to take action?		
Reasons: How do these facts support your overall message?		
For More Information: Where can your audience find more information?		

steps listed. But others, having mastered the basics, get more creative. Decisions are made based on personal preferences, time restrictions, and availability of ingredients. These cooks are able to think more strategically, weighing the tools they have at their disposal with the needs of those who will be eating. Assessment-capable visible learners are like those talented cooks in our own families. They are able to pair tools and strategies with intentions and desired outcomes.

It's difficult to make decisions and solve problems when you don't know where you are or where you're heading. The cook who knows what dish she's going to prepare is much more likely to succeed. In classrooms, learning intentions and success criteria help tremendously when it comes to setting these conditions. But students also need to be able to exert choice and make decisions about their own advancement. Student leadership in their own learning allows teachers to function more often as "activators and evaluators of learning" (Hattie, 2012, p. 186). This is different from being an evaluator of *learners*, which is about sorting them into categories.

To be sure, the tools students need to solve problems and forward their own learning must be taught, but more importantly, regularly used. Strategic applications of tools are mental and intellectual skills, not behavioral ones. Students are going to have a far more difficult time establishing learning habits if they are rarely given the opportunity to use them. Unfortunately, we often see lots of energy being expended on initial strategies instruction, but with little opportunity to use them under anything other than highly engineered circumstances. Underlining the main idea on a worksheet of paragraphs doesn't make the student any more able to determine importance. Finding the main idea shouldn't be an academic exercise. It should be a strategic tool readers use when they are trying to gain an understanding of something they are reading. Students need to use these and other strategies with purpose, in the context of learning.

Assessment-capable
visible learners are
actively engaged and
can marshal skills and
dispositions to advance
their learning.

Assessment-capable visible learners are those who are actively engaged and can marshal skills and dispositions in order to advance their learning. John speaks often of the need to bring together the skill, the will, and the thrill of learning in our classrooms. Skill is about a learner's knowledge, while will is the learner's disposition. Claxton and Lucas (2016) memorably state that "a skill is something you can do; a disposition is something you are on the look-out for opportunities to do" (p. 7). Bring skill and will together, and add motivation to learn something interesting, and now you have the third ingredient: thrill. In this chapter, we examine how assessment-capable visible learners combine skill and will by selecting learning strategies to move forward in their journey. We begin by discussing the importance of equipping students with the skills and tools they need to forward their own learning and their relationship to strategic thinking. An essential, but underutilized tool is the effect of practice on learning. We consider deliberative practice as a specific strategic tool under the student's influence. We then transition to an examination of the effectiveness of teaching cognitive study skills in order to provide students with the ability to teach themselves. Next, we will discuss the importance of problem solving as a decision-making tool for students to use. These conditions are bound up in both skill ("I know how to do something.") and will ("I want to do something."). We close out this chapter with discussion of literacy routines to create opportunities for students to apply strategic thinking in the company of their teacher and peers.

We need to bring together the skill, the will, and the thrill of learning in our classrooms.

Learning How to Learn

Study skills are a constellation of competencies that allow students to acquire, record, organize, synthesize, remember, and use information (Hoover & Patton, 1995). And who wouldn't want students to be able to do those things? They are important in learning content and they are transferable, allowing students to apply what they have learned in new situations.

QUESTIONS FOR REFLECTION

How might you give students choice over what metacognitive and cognitive strategies to use to support their learning?

Hattie (2009) suggested that study skills could be organized into three categories: *cognitive*, *meta-cognitive*, and *affective*. Cognitive study skills usually involve a task, such as note-taking or summarizing. Metacognitive study skills describe self-management, such as planning and monitoring, as well as recognizing when to use various cognitive strategies. Affective study skills involve motivation, agency, and self-concept. Figure 4.2 contains a table of study skills organized into these three categories. As Hattie notes, teaching study skills in isolation can improve students' surface learning. However, teaching study skills in concert with content area can improve deep learning. Elementary classrooms are ideal places to build study skills as students generally have the same teacher for all subjects. Thus, teachers can integrate study skills into their science, social studies, and art lessons. As students move to middle school and high school, teachers should be aware of, and integrate, study skills into their content area lessons.

Figure 4.2   Learning How to Learn

Cognitive Study Skills	Metacognitive Study Skills	Affective Study Skills
<ul><li>Note-taking and graphic organizers (creating and using)</li><li>Summarizing</li><li>Practice and rehearsal techniques (e.g., flashcards, mnemonics, memorization)</li><li>Rereading</li></ul>	<ul><li>Planning for the task</li><li>Monitoring one's learning</li><li>Reviewing and revising corrected work</li><li>Self-assessment</li><li>Self-question</li></ul>	<ul><li>Motivation to study</li><li>Structuring the environment to study</li><li>Belief in its usefulness</li><li>Agency to influence one's learning</li><li>Willingness to solve problems</li><li>Managing stress and anxiety</li><li>Goal setting</li></ul>

online resources   Available for download at **resources.corwin.com/assessment-capable**

QUESTIONS FOR REFLECTION

What kinds of study skills have your students learned?

Which do they apply?

How do you or could you support their skills?

The Effects of Practice on Learning

"You can't get good at something you don't do." Observing others doing something is important for building a model of what a skill or behavior looks like, but without intentional practice, you're not going to build your own skills. (Think of all the cooking/dancing/sports competitions you've watched.) Likewise, students need to practice academic skills in order to gain fluency and proficiency. Most teachers create opportunities for guided practice as part of their teaching. But creating assessment-capable visible learners means going a step further. Teachers need to get students to engage in intentional practice in order for them to acquire and consolidate knowledge. That means that educating students about the benefits of practice is essential. As we have stated before, assessment-capable learners are able to go above the low bar of compliance to steer their own course.

Practice is fundamental to learning, especially when acquiring and consolidating cognitive and motor skills. Most readers are familiar with Malcolm Gladwell's "10,000 hour rule" which claims that expertise arises from a time commitment to engage in practice. However, it is useful to understand that he is referring to deliberative practice, which is not simply rote rehearsal, but rather is difficult and strains the learner. In other words, it is not just *work*, but *work that is hard to do* (Ericsson, Krampe, & Tesch-Römer, 1993). A basketball player doesn't gain expertise simply by throwing countless free throws from the line in a quiet gym. He changes up the demand by practicing from different locations on the court, and tests himself as he pushes through a variety of distractions. In other words, he makes the work hard. We are reminded of a quote attributed to martial arts icon Bruce Lee: "I fear not the man who has practiced 10,000 kicks once, but I fear the man who has practiced one kick 10,000 times."

But practice is used for other purposes besides building expertise. Some practice is used to build automaticity such that something becomes increasingly fluent and requires a decreasing amount of attention. In the last chapter, we referred to the development of automaticity (LaBerge & Samuels, 1974). Automaticity comes from rehearsal and repetition. Learning multiplication facts, sight words, the periodic table of elements, significant dates and events in a nation's history—these are all examples of discrete skills and concepts that pave the way for deeper learning to occur. There are any number of rehearsal techniques that are excellent for building automaticity, such as flashcards, mnemonics, mapping, and summarizing. These and other study skills have a strong effect size ($d = 0.63$; Hattie, 2012). In fact, we think so highly of study skills instruction that we will devote a later portion of this chapter to the topic. But in terms of student factors, the fundamental question for them is being able to answer why they are practicing, in order to select the right approach.

The third-grade learners in John Kovena's class are challenged to answer this question first before selecting their activity for practicing language. Mr. Kovena explains, "The children at this school are learning to speak and read in Hopi as well as in English. Our language is our culture. We want our young people to be able to speak with their elders and participate in traditions." Mr. Kovena devotes time each day to developing his students' Hopi language skills, which includes time for practice. Before moving to collaborative and independent practice activities, they must consider their goals. *"Are you working on memorizing or on expertise?"* he asks, reminding them *"you need both. You just need to know why you're doing what you're doing."* The teacher has a number of possible activities for them to choose and labeled as either "Build

Video 4.1
Choice and
Deliberate Practice, K–5

*resources.corwin.com/
assessment-capable*

My Memory" or "Build My Expertise." Peter decides that he wants to focus on memorizing and chooses a Hopi vocabulary flashcard game to play with another classmate. Freddy has selected expertise building on this day and settles in to listen to a recording in the Hopi language of a folktale told by a volunteer. Another classmate has also selected expertise and has chosen to write a short message in Hopi in a greeting card to her grandmother, using language frames the teacher has prepared. Mr. Kovena speaks briefly with each, asking about each child's goals. Peter wants to beat his previous time naming all the vocabulary words in his deck, while Freddy will retell the folktale in Hopi to his teacher. Alice, the student writing to her grandmother, will ask Mr. Kovena to preview it for errors before sealing it in the envelope. "I wouldn't say there's anything unusual about what [the students] are doing," said the teacher. "I want them to know why and to have choice. Practice works much better when you know what you want out of it."

Make the most of practice by ensuring that it meets three conditions: *targeted*, *distributed*, and *self-directed*. Targeted practice is excellent when developing memorization through rehearsal. Repeated reading, discussed later in the chapter, is an excellent example of a targeted practice instructional strategy. Students at the health sciences-focused secondary school where two of us work compete at the state and national levels in events such as medical spelling, emergency responding, public health information campaigns, and medical photography. One event is a prepared team presentation for public health that must be timed and delivered live to sync with the wordless background video the students develop. The topic changes each year. One year the topic was the Zika virus, and a team of six high school students developed the video and scripted their lines for the five-minute speech. They engaged in weeks of targeted practice as they honed their speaking skills and timed each line. Working first with full scripts, then note cards, and finally without any supports, they timed each line so that speakers could adjust the rate of speech to pace and coordinate their delivery with the silent video in the background. Perhaps most interesting was the way they rehearsed, chunking each portion into 30-second passages. Only when they felt they had reached mastery of the first segment would they then move on to the second. Gradually, they coupled longer strings of passages until they had memorized the entire presentation. Apparently it worked, as the team took second in the state and competed in the international competition!

Mr. Kovena's decision to set aside time each day for students to practice their language skills is an example of distributed practice. Most of us have learned from our own failures that cramming for a test the night before the exam rarely delivers satisfactory results. Simply said, distributed practice is more effective than mass practice ($d = 0.71$; Hattie, 2009). It is the practice that is distributed in regular intervals over days and weeks that facilitates acquisition of new knowledge. Without regular practice, skills atrophy. Unfortunately, too many students naïvely believe that an intensive cram session of several hours is just as useful as short daily sessions leading up to an event. Eighth-grade student Victor explained it this way to his class on a presentation about learning habits:

> It's like learning to play soccer. I'm working on my dribbling skills right now. Coach sets up cones for us to perform drills. If I only practiced dribbling for a few hours before the match and didn't touch a soccer ball any other time, I'd be off the team. Same thing with studying for computer programming tests. If I try to memorize it all the night before, it's a fail.

A third condition of practice is that whenever possible it should be self-directed. Goals that have been determined by the student fuel learning in ways that those set by others cannot. A middle school team of teachers introduced Mastery Monday as a way to create opportunities for students to engage in self-directed practice. Students review the results of the previous week's work, including feedback on assignments and homework, and choose an assignment (or portion) they would like to revisit. During a 15-minute segment of the class, they revise responses and resubmit. Math teacher Beth Russell said it works especially well in her content area. "Some of the learning they experience by the end of the week is more advanced. Giving them a chance to go back and make corrections to problems from earlier in the week reinforces the learning." Student Ricardo, who had been listening to the conversation, added "I like it when I see the number correct change on the [digital] assignment," he said. "We don't get a grade on these, 'cause our course grades are competency based. We only get grades on the unit tests. But I like seeing the green bar for the number correct get higher."

Video 4.2
Choice and
Deliberate Practice, 6–12

resources.corwin.com/
assessment-capable

QUESTIONS
FOR
REFLECTION

In your content area, what type of practice builds expertise?

What type develops automaticity?

What are some ways you could incorporate practice that is targeted, distributed, and self-directed?

Teach Students How to Practice, Study, and Learn

High school teachers sometimes assume that their students have been taught to engage in study sometime earlier in their schooling. The truth is that many have not, and their lack of skill about how to do so catches up with many of them by middle school when the volume of content knowledge overwhelms them and they can no longer get by on paying attention. In this next section, we profile five cognitive study skills that can be introduced to elementary students. Of course, these are equally vital at the secondary level. However, these skills pay off when introduced early as a part of learning.

Mnemonics

A useful strategy to help with initial recall of information is mnemonics, from the Greek word for memory. You may rely on mnemonics, for instance, to recall the lines EGBDF on the treble clef ("Every Good Boy Does Fine"). Teach students this strategy to boost their recall. While learning the cardinal points of the compass, students in Michael Saunders' first-grade class were introduced to the mnemonic "Never Eat Shredded Wheat" to associate the directions in the correct order clockwise starting at the top. But as Mr. Saunders said to his class, "I really like shredded wheat, so I don't like to try to remember the directions with this saying. How about each table group come up with a different mnemonic that they can use to remember this information?" One of the groups came up with "No Evidence Sorry Writers" and another group suggested "Never Eat Shaved Walrus."

Graphic Organizers

Visually organized information can help students see connections between the ideas and information they are learning. The key to using graphic organizers as a study skill is to ensure that students are not simply copying from their teacher. Instead, students need to be given information and then encouraged to select a graphic organizer that will allow them to represent the information. For example, the students in Marco Jimenez's fourth-grade class were studying the similarities and differences between the state government and the federal government. The students had read from their textbook, watched a video, engaged in a class discussion, and heard their teacher talk about this. They had a lot of information but Mr. Jimenez knew that they wouldn't remember it, much less be able to use the information, if they didn't study it. He asked his students to think about all of the graphic organizers that they had used and to identify one that they believed would work to capture similarities and differences. Carlos chose a compare-and-contrast diagram whereas Natalie selected an attribute tool that allowed her to name each factor and then note how it was used in the state and federal government. In all, there were six different tools selected by the students in Mr. Jimenez's class.

Flashcards

This sounds very old school, but flashcards (and their digital equivalents such as Quizlet.com and the Chegg app) can help students remember information. Of course, they need to do more than remember information, but remembering is important. The third-grade students in Hiroko Mayekawa's class used a free app called StudyBlue, which allows users to create flashcards with text, pictures, and audio. During their investigation of biomes, students were focused on diverse life forms from different environments. Ms. Mayekawa asked her students to create a series of flash cards so that they could remember the various biomes, the environmental conditions of those biomes, and the types of animals that lived in the environment. In doing so, she provided her students with a lot of options about what to include and the app provided them options for how to include their information. In creating the flashcards, students were studying the biomes. And in practicing with their flashcards, they were continuing to think about the content they were expected to learn.

Summarizing

Writing summaries of content area information is another way to study. Importantly, it's not the only way that students should study, but when they write summaries about their learning, they start to chunk information in ways that they can remember. Ideally students summarize across multiple sources of information. This provides them with an opportunity to integrate ideas. Unfortunately, students often write summaries that are longer than the original sources they read and they use the exact same words as the author used. They need to be taught to summarize by identifying key words in the sources and then generating sentences on their own around the key terms. Andrea Stein teaches her sixth graders to summarize as they read. Ms. Stein models summary writing for her students before asking them to take on this task. In addition, she meets with students during their conferring time to talk about the summaries that her students have written. For example, while meeting with Jacob to talk about his summary of women in ancient civilizations, Ms. Stein says, *"How are you feeling about your summaries this week?"* And Jacob responds that he thinks that they are improving and that he is keeping focused on the main ideas. Ms. Stein agrees, adding, *"In this summary, you have three main points, the same as the author. It seems to me that was a good choice. How did you decide to do that?"* Jacob responded, *"So, I was thinking that I couldn't really leave any one of them out. I mean, some women in Greece dressed like men to go see sports. That's a detail but I think that it is important because that is different from women in Sparta."* Their conversation continued and it was obvious to Ms. Stein that Jacob's summaries helped him learn, and remember, the content of her social studies class.

Problem Solving

In addition to possessing the cognitive skills to study, students need to develop the will (motivation) to solve problems, make decisions, and take action. However, an important consideration is the gap between what the learner knows and what she needs to reach a learning goal. If the distance between what a learner currently knows and will need to know in order to resolve a problem is too great, chances are good that the learner will not be successful. In order to bridge this distance, teachers provide tools that will help students resolve problems. For example, in the opening scenario, Ms. Gregory made a variety of templates available to Alisha in order to resolve the problem of organizing information for the video they would be producing. Learners' dispositions and attitudes also play a part in whether they will successfully resolve a problem or not. Dispositions are more general in nature; for example, a learner who routinely works cooperatively with peers is likely to have a disposition toward peer learning. However, attitudes are more situational; a learner who avoids independent reading time but not other activities may be signaling that she has a negative attitude about the task (Renaud, 2013).

There are dispositions and attitudes related to problem solving as well. Dispositions needed for problem solving include the willingness to persist, to seek assistance, to be curious, and to seek answers. However, attitudes may interfere. Possessing a fixed mindset about confronting a difficult writing assignment, for instance, can narrow a student's vision for how he might go about resolving a problem. As noted in the previous chapter, one's possession of a fixed or malleable mindset is not consistent across all situations. A growth mindset is a coping strategy to draw upon in the face of challenge, and one that should not be uncoupled from effort and outcomes (Dweck, 2016). Therefore, the amount of scaffolding and feedback needed about how the problem is being solved is likely to vary for each child and across content areas. Learners need teachers who are responsive to their needs and ensure that they experience enough success to build confidence and help them clarify their thinking. Clear and shared understandings of what success looks like helps to develop dispositions and attitudes for accepting greater levels of challenge.

Fifth-grade student Neil isn't very confident about his ability in his science class, especially in labs that involve a lot of data to analyze. The good news is that his teacher, Eileen Viterbo, is working at fostering his problem-solving skills. During a lab on magnets in which he needed to draw conclusions about the relationship between the strength of electromagnets and the number of wraps of insulated copper wire around a nail, Neil faltered. Noting his distress, Ms. Viterbo stopped by Neil's lab table and began asking him what he knew so far, inviting him to list his findings. Within a few minutes, Neil had correctly surmised that his data showed that more windings were equated with a stronger electromagnet. She then reframed what he had done to resolve the problem:

I want you to see how you followed scientific procedures to answer your investigation. First, you conducted multiple trials and only changed one variable, which was the number of windings. You recorded your findings in a table so you could see the results. Then you analyzed the data by looking for a pattern. You found that the more copper windings were on the nail, the more iron shavings your electromagnet could pick up. You solved this problem because you followed a system. Trust yourself!

At that last remark, Neil smiled. *"I know, Ms. Viterbo, it's like you always say: Just breathe and think like a scientist!"*

Fostering the dispositions and attitudes of students to take on their own learning is a primary job of any caring educator. However, these must be a part of the fabric of the classroom, not simply isolated lessons on "persistence" and "mindset" that are divorced from any context (Claxton & Lucas, 2016). These dispositions and attitudes are either built or destroyed each time we speak to a child, notice or ignore nonverbal signals of distress, mark student papers, and fill out report cards. We communicate what is important and what is not valued through these interactions. Teaching is never solely about knowledge building. Each interaction is an opportunity to strengthen a learner's habits for planning, organizing, and resolving problems. A consistent focus on performance of learning (grades), rather than mastery (learning) in turn can undermine even young children's mindsets, including those who began the school year with a positive motivational framework about their own learning (Daeun, Gunderson, Eli, Levine, & Beilock, 2016).

> Fostering the dispositions and attitudes of students to take on their own learning is a primary job of any caring educator. These dispositions and attitudes are either built or destroyed each time we speak to a child, notice or ignore nonverbal signals of distress, mark student papers, and fill out report cards.

Create Opportunities to Apply Strategies

We are not suggesting that learning is about squirreling oneself away in an isolated corner. Much of the enactment of strategic thinking comes in the company of others, both teacher and peers, especially through meaningful discussion. Learning in the company of others, and with others, deepens and extends what a learner can soon do independently. Reading is an example of an academic pursuit that is usually defined as a wholly internalized act, yet in the classroom is rightly developed in a sociocultural context. Reading comprehension strategies instruction has been of singular interest for decades, most notably through a series of studies examining what good readers do (e.g., Paris, Lipson, & Wixson, 1983). These strategic readers make conscious and deliberate plans, such as making connections to prior knowledge, forming and revising predictions, and employing mental visualizations as needed. But a criticism is that these strategies have been turned into curriculum itself. Instead of applying these approaches as needed to increasingly complex texts, they are taught and retaught for years, often as discrete units. Once students have initially learned about ways to monitor their understanding, for instance, they don't need to be introduced to it again. Rather, they need opportunities to use them authentically during the act of reading.

Collaborative Reasoning

Once taught, comprehension strategies are evidenced in discussions of texts. These collaborative conversations provide students with opportunities to apply critical thinking. Collaborative reasoning is a peer-led small group protocol for fostering critical analysis skills (Zhang & Stahl, 2011). The teacher is present to facilitate the discussion, which often begins with a "big question" that is meant to encourage a critical stance. Second-grade students in Janelle Lowe's class had read an informational article on a community garden in their city. The protocol she uses, developed by Clark et al. (2003) can be found in Figure 4.3. During the small group discussion that followed, Ms. Lowe began by asking her students, *"Why does this community work?"* Her students, who have been studying communities in social studies, use the article to critically analyze the text:

Jamal: *The people in this garden did all kinds of stuff.*

Trina: *Like they weren't all the same . . .*

Jamal: *Yeah, like some of the people was old, and then there was bigger kids, too.*

Anisa: *But they all helped. Like the big kids carried heavy stuff . . .*

Trina: *An' little kids pulled weeds. I pull weeds in my Mama's garden.*

Ms. Lowe: *You are saying that people of different ages worked in the garden.*

Kendall: *It's like a family.*

Ms. Lowe: *Say more about that.*

Kendall: *Families have old people and babies and kids and grownups.*

Trina: . . . and so do neighborhood communities.

Jamal: In the community garden, everyone has a job.

Ms. Lowe: Why is that important for a community?

Anisa: 'Cause then everyone is needed.

Ms. Lowe's use of collaborative reasoning is an extension of her small group guided-reading routine. Collaborative reasoning provides her students with the opportunity to think critically, and to engage in discussion that is driven by the voices of their peers rather than a conventional questioning routine that can limit thinking.

Figure 4.3   Seven Steps for Collaborative Reasoning Discussions

1. After the class reads the text, small groups come together for a discussion.
2. The teacher poses a central question concerning a dilemma faced by a character in the story.
3. Students freely explain their positions on the central question to the members of their group.
4. They expand on their ideas, adding reasons and supporting evidence from the story and everyday experience.
5. They challenge each other's thinking and ways of reasoning.
6. At the end of the discussion, a final poll is taken to see where everyone stands.
7. Finally, the teacher and students review the discussion and make suggestions on how to improve future discussions.

Source: Clark, A. M., Anderson, R. C., Kuo, L., Kim, I. H., Archodidou, A., & Nguyen-Jahiel, K. (2003). Collaborative reasoning: Expanding ways for children to talk and think in school. Educational Psychology Review, 15(2), 181–198.

Repeated Reading

Repeated reading is another sound practice for deepening reading skills, although one that is unfortunately misused by many well-meaning teachers. Repeated reading is an instructional method first articulated by Samuels (1979). In its original form, repeated reading required a short passage of 50 to 200 words, read several times silently and aloud until sufficient levels of rate and accuracy were attained. Later efforts included corrective feedback from an adult, as well as student goal setting and self-monitoring of progress. Repeated reading instruction has been extensively researched. A number of studies on repeated reading have been further analyzed using a statistical tool called a meta-analysis, which is used to calculate effect size across multiple studies. Therrien's (2004) meta-analysis of 16 studies is widely cited and offers interesting information beyond the positive impact of repeated reading. This study revealed several essential instructional conditions, namely that repeated reading (1) is performed in the company of an adult who reads the passage first, (2) requires that the text be read 3 to 4 times by the child, and (3) involves corrective feedback. A more recent meta-analysis of 34 studies on the effects of repeated reading instruction for elementary students with learning disabilities confirms these results. Lee and Yoon (2017) found that it was especially beneficial in building fluency, which was further enhanced when students were able to listen to the text being read before reading it themselves. Hattie (2012) found that repeated reading instruction provides an effect size of 0.67, equivalent to approximately 1.5 years of growth for a year in school.

But repeated reading has the potential for building more than fluency and comprehension—it can build the habit of rereading. Rereading behaviors and repeated reading draw on two related constructs. The first, rereading, is a habit that ultimately is under the direction of the student. The second, repeated reading is an instructional routine devised to build fluency and comprehension. Underpinning both is the element of repetition. These practices, while implemented somewhat differently, have similar goals.

Rereading to clarify understanding of a text is a tool students can utilize. However, they need authentic reasons to reread, not just for compliance. Changing the task and purpose provides students an authentic reason for rereading.

Assessment-capable visible learners understand that rereading to clarify understanding of a text is a tool they can utilize. However, they need authentic reasons to reread, not just for compliance. Teachers of young children who are at the emergent stage of reading can reference the print more often during shared readings with picture books. Questions that reference print are especially important for emergent readers, who do not naturally attend to print. Evans, Williamson, and Pursoo (2008) found that young children only looked at print during shared readings 6% of the time. Without questions that draw their attention to the print and linguistic features of the text, students fail to learn the value of rereading to bolster their understanding, relying instead on what they knew prior to, or can recall from, the shared reading. This can privilege auditory memory over investigation and evidence from the text.

Changing the task and purpose provides students an authentic reason for rereading. During a shared reading with the picture book, *On a Beam of Light* (Berne, 2013), first-grade teacher Monica Ramos introduced the text, saying, *"I'm going to read about a famous scientist named Albert Einstein. The first time I read it will be so you can get some ideas about his life."*

After finishing the book, she said, *"Now we're going to read it a second time, and this time I want you to listen and look for evidence that tells us if this story could be true."* Her change of purpose for reading helped her students focus on the nonfiction elements of the narrative. Her students agreed that the bulk of the book could have been fiction, but the last page offered information about his discoveries. *"Show me where you found that?"* the teacher asked. A student replied, *"It says right here* [pointing] *about the moon and about spaceships."* Focusing on print references, the teacher then said, *"Can you touch the word on this page that says* moon?"

The students in Greg Leong's sixth-grade English class were reading *Wonder* (Palacio, 2012). Much of the reading and discussion of the novel occurred in small group literature circles, but the teacher reserved some passages for a closer inspection of the text. One such passage occurred about one-third of the way through the book, involving the character Auggie's older sister Olivia. Auggie has a severe birth defect, and his sister recalls waking up one night to see her mother standing outside Auggie's room watching him sleep. After inviting students to read the passage silently, he asks them to read it again, this time to annotate. Each student had a personal copy of the text and the teacher said, *"Here's what I want you to focus on this time. The author spends half of this passage using descriptive language about the way Auggie's mother looked as she stood in the hall. Make a note in the margin of your book about how the author paints this picture with words. Then we'll discuss it together."* In both of these cases, the teachers provided authentic reasons for students to reread by changing the purpose and the task.

Mr. Leong understands the value of repeated reading, but knows that his students will be resistant if they don't see a purpose. He also knows that audience and performance are authentic motivators for rereading text because they offer a purpose for doing so. One method of providing an audience is reader's theater, which requires two or more readers to perform the text aloud. Unlike a conventional theater performance, the script remains present and other elements such as props, movement, and lighting are absent. The purpose is to use authentic practice to build oral reading fluency, prosody, and comprehension, all the while keeping eyes on text. Martinez, Roser, and Strecker (1998) documented its use with second-grade students who participated in five-day sequences of reader's theater. The researchers documented ways these small groups made meaning of the script, noting that "students themselves initiated discussion regarding oral interpretation that delved into comprehension on a deep level" and returning to the text to reach consensus on details of the performance (p. 332).

Mr. Leong used a reader's theater technique to bring dialogue-heavy passages to life. "I want them to 'hear' these characters in their heads as they read," he explained. "The dialogue is rich, funny, and sometimes poignant. I'm also teaching about direct and indirect characterization right now, and dialogue is one important example of the author's craft."

One passage occurs late in *Wonder*, after Auggie and four friends narrowly escape a beating by some older boys. The teacher met with the five students who would be performing this for the class later in the week. *"So you've read this and you understand how it fits into the plot. But let's talk about their emotions, and how the author shows this,"* said the teacher. *"Well, they're relieved that they got away,"* said one student. *"And they're all pumped up, too,"* added another.

"But how do you know? Can you go back into the text to figure out where you're getting that impression?" asked the teacher. Using a scripted version of the passage, the students and their teacher annotate the evidence, including punctuation marks, phrases like "we all started laughing" and the author's descriptions about the characters trading high-fives and being out of breath from running. Satisfied that the group is on their way to capturing the emotional heart of the passage, he leaves them to work out tracking the dialogue, assigning roles, and beginning rehearsals. Two days later, the group performed it using their "radio voices" to bring the scene to life.

Conclusion

It's not enough to "cover the content." Instead, teachers have to focus on the ways in which people learn content, which includes practice and feedback.

Assessment-capable visible learners know where they're headed and have tools for the journey. These tools are a set of metacognitive and cognitive strategies that propel their learning, especially when faced with challenge. It is important that students are taught about effective tools, but it's probably even more important that they come to understand a few things about these tools, namely

- Not all tools work for all problems

- They have choice over which tools to use

- They should replace tools that are not working

Developing students' understanding of these principles requires that teachers provide them with multiple opportunities to try on learning tools. That means that learners need to make decisions about which strategies to select. In addition, as students increase the responsibility they have for their own learning, teachers must provide students with the means for students to assess their own learning and then to make adjustments in their learning plans, which might include the selection of new or different tools.

In this vein, study skills and deliberate practice become important considerations for teaching. It's not enough to "cover the content." Instead, teachers have to focus on the ways in which people learn content, which includes practice and feedback. Coupled with the affective dispositions these learners depend upon, the outcome of these efforts will be the development of students who can tap into the skill, will, and thrill of learning.

ASSESSMENT–CAPABLE VISIBLE LEARNERS...
Seek Feedback and Recognize That Errors Are Opportunities to Learn

"I'm going to read this to Denise. Writers have to know what their audience thinks."

Third-grade student Larissa has put the finishing touches on an imaginative story she has written about three ghosts that solve a mystery in a haunted house and is seeking the feedback of her writing partner, Denise. Her class has been reading mysteries, including selections from *Cam Jansen* (Adler, 2004) and the *Encyclopedia Brown* (Sobel, 2007) series, and she's anxious to try out her hand with the genre. Larissa and her classmates had planned their mysteries, first figuring out the problem to be solved, the suspects, and who would be the detective in the story. Larissa had also learned about the elements of a good mystery, such as having clues that add up in the end, and making sure a distraction in the story would lead readers in a false direction. "It all has to make sense," explained Larissa.

Students in her class regularly collaborate as writing partners, reading each other's drafts to provide feedback. Larissa's teacher, Marlene Carlson, created a rubric for writing partners to use to guide their feedback (see Figure 5.1). "This isn't evaluative," said Ms. Carlson. "There's no score. What each partner is reading for is to see if the mystery has a logical flow." Larissa points out the last element on the rubric, labeled *Next Steps*:

A student who can't give accurate feedback is probably a student who doesn't understand yet what success looks like.

The next thing we do after we meet with our writing partner is we meet with the teacher. Denise's feedback should give her [Larissa] a clear idea about what she needs to accomplish next in her writing. And it really helps me because I can spend my time focused on the support that's needed, rather than starting all over. Plus, it gives me an idea of who's giving accurate feedback, and who needs more guidance. A student who can't give accurate feedback is probably a student who doesn't understand yet what success looks like.

Larissa, Denise, and the other students in Ms. Carlson's class are building their capacity to become assessment-capable visible learners. They are learning the value of being able to gauge their own progress, rather than only relying on the single adult in the room to tell them when they are successful. As diligent as Ms. Carlson is, she can't possibly provide enough timely and specific feedback to each student. She knows she needs to enlist her students in this effort. That means that her students need to develop the internal ability to attend to their own progress, and learn to seek feedback from others to make corrections and continue to grow and learn. This doesn't just happen, so

Ms. Carlson also understands that she must teach these skills and create opportunities for students to practice them. Assessment-capable visible learners thrive with useful feedback from three sources: self, peers, and teachers.

Figure 5.1 Mystery Writing Rubric for Elementary Grades

Mystery Writer's Name: _____

Mystery Reader's Name: _____

	Sleuth!	Tracker	Back to the Drawing Board
Plot	The plot has a strong beginning, middle, and ending that I can follow.	Most of the plot makes sense, but I have some questions.	I'm confused!
Characters	The characters are described in detail.	Some characters are described in detail, but others are confusing.	Not sure who is in the story or why!
Clues	There are clues that make sense.	Some clues are there, but others are missing.	The clues didn't add up!
Distractions	There was a good distraction that threw me off the trail!	There was a distraction, but I could figure it out right away.	There was no distraction to keep me on my toes.
Solution	Everything made sense at the end!	Most of the solutions made sense, but I still have questions.	The mystery wasn't solved in a way I could understand.
What's Next	Meet next with Ms. Carlson to polish your story.	Meet next with Ms. Carlson to work out the bugs.	Meet next with Ms. Carlson to tighten up your mystery.

online resources ↘ Available for download at **resources.corwin.com/assessment-capable**

Video 5.1
Creating Opportunities
for Feedback

resources.corwin.com/
assessment-capable

Feedback needs to be
timely, specific, and
actionable, meaning
that students can
apply the feedback to
revise their work.

In this chapter, we will shine a spotlight on feedback as a catalyst for learning. The type of feedback teachers provide, however well meaning, can in fact inhibit learning, so it is crucial to understand how to best leverage this powerful tool. Next, we will profile teachers who create opportunities for feedback to occur from the three sources we have noted: self, peers, and teachers. Feedback dovetails into the last element we address in this chapter, which is the importance of errors and challenge as a necessary condition of learning. No one relishes making errors, but the stance we adopt in understanding the vital nature of errors can spell the difference between an assessment-capable visible learner and one who plays it safe.

Feedback Fuels Learning

Students who reliably gauge their own progress are receptive to receiving copious amounts of feedback. They can use their own feedback loop by engaging in reflective self-questioning, thereby becoming more metacognitively aware. Their peers are another source of feedback, particularly as they engage in peer critiques. And teachers are a major source for feedback. But not all feedback is useful. First, it needs to be timely. It's remarkable how quickly feedback gets stale. In addition, it should be specific and actionable, meaning that students can apply the feedback to revise their work. Saving your very best feedback for the summative assignment is a waste of your time and theirs, if students don't have an opportunity to act upon it.

With all the emphasis on feedback, it is important to note that the ultimate arbiter of its usefulness is the receiver, not the giver (Hattie, 2011). It is the student who determines whether it is understandable, which means the teacher must be attuned to feedback language. If a student doesn't understand the feedback a teacher gives, then it isn't useful. Period. Perceptions about feedback are influenced by cultural and personal factors specific to the learner, to be sure. However, a major factor is the relationship the student has with the teacher. Zumbrunn, Marrs, and Mewborn's (2016) examination of middle and high school students' perceptions of feedback about their writing noted that students' relationship to the teacher had a mediating effect. While a majority of the student respondents (80%) said they liked receiving feedback about their writing, 20% did not. Among those who had a negative perception, 65% of student comments disregarded the source of the feedback (the teacher) and expressed indifference to the value of feedback for them (p. 361):

- "If I'm happy with my writing, their opinion doesn't matter."

- "It's annoying."

- "I don't really care."

- "I'm really not interested in getting feedback."

- "Some teachers are mean."

- "I don't like writing and [teachers] are really critical so I just say whatever and keep writing."

Importantly, the researchers found that low self-efficacy about writing also had bearing in student perceptions about feedback. They noted that "if improving student writing self-regulation is a goal, then it becomes important to not only provide feedback on students' writing, but also on their strategy use" (p. 363). Consistent with other studies about student perceptions of feedback, the middle and high school students in this study who felt negatively about their writing did not see teacher comments as an avenue to becoming better writers. A related study of elementary students drew similar conclusions. Children drew pictures of themselves writing in the classroom and discussed their perceptions. Negative perceptions of some students cited isolation from the teacher, and those students stated that they experienced anxiety or physical or emotional pain about their writing (Zumbrunn, Ekholm, Stringer, McKnight, & DeBusk-Lane,2017).

At its best, feedback should help students become more consciously aware of what they are doing, their decisions for doing so, and what problem-solving strategies and processes they can use to correct, revise, or improve their work. It isn't enough to provide instruction on strategies; we must link them to the self-regulation the learners can exercise to gauge their progress and move forward. Feedback is the link between the two.

A Model of Feedback

Feedback has been described as the most underutilized instructional approach teachers have at their disposal. Teachers will often say that they know feedback is useful, but they offer *useful* feedback surprisingly infrequently, with most incidents consisting of general praise of a nonspecific nature (*"You've done a fantastic job!"*), and usually only one or two sentences in length (Voerman, Meijer, Korthagen, & Simons, 2012). It truly is a lost opportunity as well, since the effect size of feedback is 0.73 (Hattie, 2012). Perhaps it is so effective because it encapsulates so many of the sound approaches detailed throughout this book. The purpose of feedback should remain constant—to progressively close the gap between present and desired

Video 5.2
Providing Specific and
Actionable Feedback

*resources.corwin.com/
assessment-capable*

The purpose of feedback
should remain constant—
to progressively close the
gap between present and
desired performance.

performance (Hattie, 2009). In order to do so, the teacher and the student must have

- The ability to determine the present level of performance (Chapter 2)

- A clear and shared understanding of the learning intentions and success criteria (Chapter 3)

- Strategies and processes that can be put into action (Chapter 4)

- Ways to gauge next steps to move forward (Chapter 6)

Figure 5.2 illustrates a model of feedback for providing feedback to students, and in turn gaining feedback from them. After all, students' work, their understandings, questions, misconceptions, and errors are all feedback to us about our own performance. Therefore, feedback should not be viewed as a one-way transmission model, but as one that operates between teacher and student.

Narrowing the gap between current performance and desired outcome requires both teacher and student. The teacher helps the student using feedback, and the student increases efforts through the application of problem-solving strategies.

Three Big Questions Your Feedback Should Address

Remember that the usefulness of the feedback is in the eye of the beholder. Therefore, the feedback we provide should address the three major questions learners have:

- Where am I going?

- How am I going there?

- Where will I go next?

The first question is addressed through the learning intentions and success criteria. Feedback from knowing what success looks like allows students to strive along with the teacher to these goals. If the goal, for example, is to write a detailed explanation of factors leading to the failure of the Fukushima Daiichi nuclear reactor in 2011, omitting information from prior safety studies would be an error that would need to be corrected. That's exactly what chemistry teacher Dennis Eagleton did when he met with his student Sharla to discuss her first draft. *"I read your draft last night. You're off to a great start,"* he began. *"Let's look at this together so we can figure out how best to support your next draft."* After identifying strengths in her

Figure 5.2   A Model of Feedback

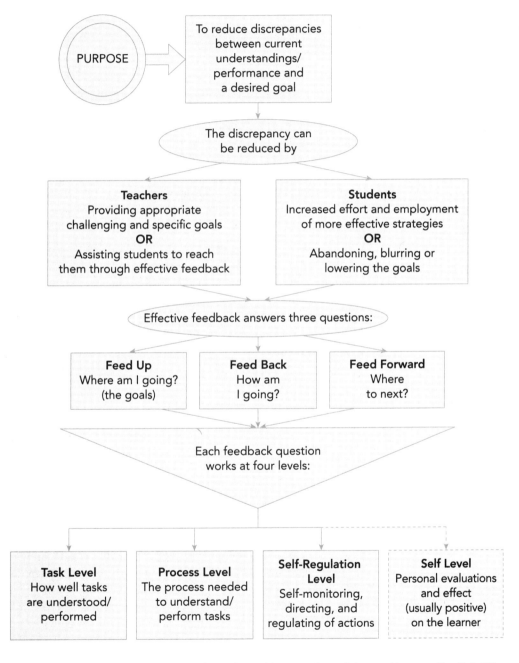

Source: Hattie, J. (2009). Visible learning: A synthesis of over 800 meta-analyses relating to achievement. New York, NY: Routledge.

initial report ("*You provided an account of the disaster at the beginning of the paper, which set the context for understanding its magnitude.*"), he turned his attention to the checklist for the report. "*What's missing so far is information about any safety concerns prior to the disaster.*"

Mr. Eagleton then went on to address the second question, which concerns using strategies to address discrepancies. "*So let's talk for a few minutes about where you might locate this information. Making a list of places to check out is going to prevent you from forgetting the ideas we brainstorm.*" He and Sharla spend a few minutes discussing possibilities, including checking the Japanese Nuclear Safety Commission and International Atomic Energy Agency websites for information. Because the students in his class were researching nuclear disasters from around the world, including Chernobyl and Three Mile Island, he had curated several such resources on his course learning management system (LMS). However, Sharla had overlooked these resources when developing her initial draft.

Mr. Eagleton then shifted his focus to the third question, addressing Sharla's next steps. "*What's next for you? It's important that you have a plan. What two or three things are you going to do?*"

Sharla offered, "*Well, I've got some reading to do for looking for any safety reports, but once I write up that part I'm going to have someone else who's not working on Fukushima read it just to make sure it makes sense.*" And smiling, she said, "*I guess I need to use the checklist a little better, too. Thanks, Mr. E!*" With that, Sharla headed back to her research team.

Four Types of Feedback

We don't mean to oversimplify feedback by reducing it to a three-step process, but rather to use it as a frame to make the feedback as useful as possible. For many students, if there is no "where-to-next" feedback then they often say they received no feedback. Of course, if this where-to-next feedback is based on feedback about the other two questions, all the better. Depending on the student and the need, feedback may address one or more of four different types. These types of feedback are typically interwoven among the three questions. The first type is feedback about the task or product. This type of feedback is sometimes called corrective feedback, as it provides information about accuracy or completeness of the assignment. Mr. Eagleton used this type of feedback to highlight what Sharla had included (context) and what she had omitted (safety concerns prior to the event). Mr. Eagleton also provided a second type of feedback, which was about processes. In his case, he focused on strategies, especially in identifying possible resources for her to use. The teacher included a third type of feedback, which concerns self-regulation. He asked Sharla about what she would do to support her own critique of her written draft, and she noted that she would consult the checklist a bit more closely and have a peer read her next version to see if it made sense.

Notice that he did not make the mistake of confining his feedback to the fourth type of feedback, which is about oneself. These often take the form of praise, usually general and vague. Telling Sharla, "*You're off to a good start!*" without any further information is not helpful to her, and would have indicated that the teacher himself hadn't thought deeply about the student's work. We are not suggesting that students should never be praised. But self-efficacy is about confidence in one's capacity and capability. Self-efficacy is drawn from knowing about the specifics, including what has already been accomplished, and what should occur next.

We mentioned before that feedback goes both ways, and Mr. Eagleton is attuned to this concept. He kept an informal tally of the errors he saw most commonly so that he could plan for some reteaching the following day. He told the class,

> *I talked to several of you who hadn't made use of the checklist before submitting it to the LMS. Tonight I'm going to change the online protocol so that you can submit a completed checklist with your draft. That should help. I'm also going to update the resources I have online. Several students mentioned great resources they used that were not on the LMS. I made a list and I'm going to add them so that others can use them. I'll review the new resources at the beginning of class tomorrow.*

Create Feedback Opportunities

Feedback opportunities need to be planned as carefully as the instruction you offer. Feedback comes from three sources: self, peers, and the teacher. But in the rush of busy classrooms, feedback opportunities are at risk of being pushed aside as other competing demands are allowed to take precedent. We're using "allowed" quite intentionally. Feedback forms the heart of the learning community. Instruction from the teacher simply can't be allowed to consume 59 minutes of every hour. Achieving some balance can actually speed up the learning. Keep in mind that effect size—0.73. The payoff in accelerated student learning is well worth the time invested in creating opportunities for feedback to occur.

Self-Reflection Feedback Loop

Maurice Evans, the twelfth-grade English teacher, talked about "pushing the pause button" after a warm-up discussion about a controversial topic. He provided students with a short writing opportunity to collect their

Video 5.3
Teaching Students to Assess Their Own Learning

resources.corwin.com/ assessment-capable

thoughts after hearing the initial ideas of one another before continuing. Other related methods include an entrance ticket. After introducing the learning intention, fourth-grade teacher Hannah Birch regularly asks her students about how much they believe they know about the topic and then asks them to return to their self-assessment at the end of the lesson. "Students are usually surprised about their estimates of their own knowledge going in," she said. "It's hard to know what you don't know, and so this is a good reminder to keep tuned in even when they think they already know it all," she smiled. Simply adding before- and after-task reflective questions can provoke more self-questioning about students' knowledge and their learning.

Peer Feedback Loop

The use of peers can provide learners with another avenue for gauging their individual progress. Third-grade budding mystery writer Larissa had learned the value of having her friend Denise react to her story to see if the clues made sense. Importantly, it was her teacher, Marlene Carlson, who had built this element into the process. Peer reviews are often utilized in classrooms as an intermediate step for receiving feedback. One of these reviews, Peer-Assisted Reflection (PAR), discussed in detail in Chapter 7, is used to help math students work through and explain their reasoning on complex math problems. Amy Miles introduces a peer critique process at the beginning of the year for all of her sixth- and seventh-grade English students. "Many of my students are English learners," she explained. Being able to offer a critique of someone's work builds their academic language skills and fosters their ability in turn to be able to critique their own work. Ms. Miles teaches language frames and guiding questions for students to use when they meet online or face-to-face to provide feedback. She has divided the frames into two major sections—content and structure—and further segmented the feedback into specific strengths and gaps or areas for growth. The frames are stored in clear plastic protectors and are readily available at each table in the classroom so that students can easily consult them as needed. There's no expectation that all of the language frames are used, or that all the guiding questions are consulted to prepare for the review. Rather, students in Ms. Miles classes select as needed and as the situation warrants. Her language frames and guiding questions can be found in Figure 5.3 on pages 86–87.

Teacher Feedback Loop

In many ways, this might be the most challenging feedback opportunity of all, because it's easy to quickly feel outnumbered. In classrooms of 30 or more, managing time while managing the classroom can be overwhelming. Classroom organizational structures can help to organize time. Elementary classrooms often use a workshop model several times a week as part of their reading/language arts block. This organizational structure provides for specific time when the teacher is conferring with individual students about their progress in reading and writing. While other students are independently reading or writing, the teacher meets with a handful of students each time. Secondary classrooms may not utilize a workshop model but can similarly devote time to confer with individual students while others are working in collaborative small groups and during independent learning. Keep in mind that it is unrealistic to expect that a single teacher could possibly provide individual feedback to each student every time. Having said that, the inability to meet with everyone in a single class period should not be an excuse for never conferring. Think of it this way: Distributed practice is more effective than mass practice. Rather than try to cram a semester's worth of feedback into a single period, schedule weekly feedback sessions to meet regularly with a smaller number of students. Done regularly, these conferences add up and provide additional valuable data when meeting more formally with parents and students.

Second-grade teacher Samuel Obaje uses his conference notes when he meets with families. "I like for the meetings to actively involve students," he explained. "The conference notes are a good record for both the student and me to consult when we talk to Mom and Dad." Mr. Obaje includes a section on his note-taking form for students to add their goals and commitments for their next steps. "It's a good accountability measure for both of us to make sure we follow up with the commitments we made to each other," said the teacher. "I need to make sure that my kids know I'm holding myself accountable, not just them."

Soliciting Feedback

How do you know when to seek feedback? To use an example from our professional lives, it is likely that you have had to write an email to someone that needed to be carefully worded. Did you send a draft of the email to someone else you trusted to screen it in advance before sending it to the intended person? If so, you sought feedback. Perhaps you did so because the information was complex and you wanted to be sure it was accurate and complete before sending it out. Alternatively, you were unsure whether your intended tone matched the message and needed to confirm that the message was not misinterpreted as being harsh, flippant, or discouraging. You may have had doubts about whether email was the right communication channel. Would it be better, you asked, to pick up the phone to discuss the situation with the intended recipient? In any case, you sought feedback because experience and the ability to self-question led you to seek help from a third party.

Figure 5.3 Language Frames for Peer Critiques

Content: The "What"

Content Strengths

Provide specific feedback to your peers regarding their strengths in content, the information being presented.

What should they continue to do?

Content Gaps or Room for Growth

Provide specific feedback to your peers regarding gaps or room for improvement in content, the information being presented.

How can they take this to the next level?

Language Frames

1. I appreciate your choice in _____ because _____.
   (type of information that was presented)

   _____
   (how providing this specific information strengthened their writing)

2. When you said "_____," it strengthened
   (their exact words)

   your argument because _____.
   (why those exact words made a difference)

3. The reader can tell that you _____
   (what message was clearly conveyed)

   due to the addition/elaboration of _____.
   (details or examples that were provided)

1. Although you incorporated/mentioned _____
   (type of information that was presented)

   as a scholar, I would recommend _____.
   (how the choice of information could have been better)

   in order to _____.
   (how this information would add to or strengthen the writing)

2. You were clear that _____;
   (information that was presented clearly)

   however, one might be led to believe _____
   (message that goes against the argument or statement)

   because you mentioned "_____."
   (their exact words that may cause confusion)

Questions to Guide Content Review

Purpose of the Writing: What are they saying?

Did they address the prompt?

What is their argument? Is their stance clear?

What information is being presented?

What do they want me to know/learn/agree with?

Do they focus on this argument throughout their writing?

Do they discuss any ideas that would be considered irrelevant or off topic?

Justification and Reasoning: Do they justify their argument or explain their reasoning?

Are they providing relevant examples or facts or is it all opinion based?

Do they offer the most appropriate textual evidence for support?

Did they explain their choice in textual evidence or examples?

Did they elaborate on anything for further understanding?

Content: The "What"

Structure Strengths

Provide specific feedback to your peers regarding their strengths in structure, how the information is presented.

What should they continue to do?

Structure Gaps or Room for Growth

Provide specific feedback to your peers regarding gaps or room for improvement in structure, how the information is being presented.

How can they take this to the next level?

Language Frames

1. The presentation of your argument is _____ (adjective with a positive connotation)

because _____ (structural component that led to this description).

2. I notice that _____ (strong understanding and use of structural component)

which looks scholarly because _____ (why this looks professional).

3. Your choice in language such as "_____" (college-bound word or phrase) really _____ because _____

_____ (what it does to the writing) (explanation of why it does this).

1. This is a great start; however, by _____ (action to take for improvement)

in the future, your writing _____ (how your writing is affected).

2. I noticed you _____ (specific statement, or idea of their writing)

and this would look/sound more professional if you were

to _____ because _____
(specific action to take) (the result in their writing from addressing this)

3. As an English scholar, I recommend _____ (what practice you recommend for writing)

because _____
(why this is important for their particular writing)

Questions to Guide Content Review

How It Looks: What stands out right away?

Did they use correct spelling, capitalization, and punctuation?

Did they indent for new paragraphs and use proper spacing?

How It Sounds: When reading out loud, what do you notice?

Were there any sections that I needed to reread?

Were they consistent with the tense of their writing?

(past: –ed / present: –ing / future: –will, would)

Did they use the proper verb tense? (*The dogs jump. vs. The dog jumps.*)

Did they repeat any words or sentences?

Do any of their ideas seem out of order?

When reading, did I run out of breath?

Reader Engagement

Did they choose the most scholarly language?

Was the tone of the writing clear?

Source: © Amy Miles, 2016, Health Sciences High and Middle College Inc.

An essential aspect of self-questioning and goal setting is in seeking feedback and help as needed. Interestingly, help seeking is not associated with helplessness, but rather with empowerment and capacity building (Butler, 1998). In fact, help avoidance is associated with a host of negative learning outcomes, including lower achievement levels, unproductive "wheel spinning" (repeatedly getting something wrong), and poor ability to make accurate judgments about one's learning (Almeda, Baker, & Corbett, 2017). Help-seeking behaviors of students include asking for explanations to clarify understanding, and seeking resources to support their learning.

But students don't always seek help or feedback from their teachers. Butler and Shibaz (2014) examined the function of positive student–teacher relationships in help seeking, noting that "whether students turn to a particular teacher depends crucially on whether they believe that the teacher cares about their students' welfare" (p. 50). This makes sense, of course. Any one of us is unlikely to seek help, no matter how much we may be aware of our own needs, from someone who does not appear to be all that caring.

Help seeking is at the core of soliciting feedback and involves both the academic and social climate. Assessment-capable visible learners reliably and regularly seek feedback about their learning and progress toward goals. But in order for students to seek feedback, teachers need to create the conditions that can allow this to flourish. That means building and maintaining a strong and caring climate of learning in the classroom, one in which students know they can approach teachers and classmates to get feedback.

> For students to seek feedback, teachers need to create the conditions that can allow this to flourish. That means building and maintaining a strong and caring climate of learning in the classroom, one in which students know they can approach teachers and classmates to get feedback.

First-grade teacher Whitney Ellison strives to create a community of learners. One method she uses is the bus stop, which is simply a sign on the wall. "There are times every day when we're doing some independent tasks. But not everyone's ready," the teacher explained. "After I give directions for the task, students evaluate their own confidence in their ability to complete it successfully. They have a go at it, but if they need feedback, there's a place for them to turn. I open up the bus stop, and people who need some additional help can simply stand over by the sign. Our job as a class is to 'pick up' anyone at the bus stop to lend a hand." The teacher also monitors the bus stop and is there to provide additional assistance as needed.

One's willingness to seek feedback is influenced by prior knowledge. Students with higher levels of prior knowledge seek feedback about processes and understanding solutions, while those with lower prior knowledge seek low-level feedback about whether an answer is correct or not (Almeda et al., 2017). Sixth-grade math teacher Shekar Arya uses a variation of worked examples during small group math instruction to foster peer feedback. After posing a problem, his students attempt to solve it independently. Mr. Arya examines each of the solutions, then selects his "favorite no"—an incorrect answer that contains some good mathematical thinking. "I give the incorrect solution back to the student, and encourage him or her to confer with the other students to do two things. The first is to figure out where the error occurred, and the second is to determine why I selected it as my favorite no," he explained. Mr. Arya enjoys listening to the feedback they give one another, especially how they offer explanations, ask clarifying questions, and speculate about the mathematical reasoning demonstrated. "As a teacher, I get two things out of it. First, I get to listen for the sophistication of their critical thinking. But the second is that I can coach them to get even better at peer feedback. I want them to pursue more than the correct answer. I want them to see the value in what they can offer one another."

QUESTIONS FOR REFLECTION

Feedback is described in this chapter as "the most underutilized approach we as teachers have at our disposal."

What are some of your areas of success and areas for growth in your use of feedback with students?

Perseverance is affected as well. Feedback fuels perseverance by providing students additional avenues of support and alternatives to the futile "wheel spinning" that effort alone cannot overcome. We believe this is an overlooked element in the conversations about persistence. An emphasis on perseverance, growth mindset, grit, or any related construct, without an equally robust commitment to creating the conditions for help seeking and feedback, will not deliver promised results. Persistence and feedback go hand in hand, and fostering the former means that we must furnish the latter.

> Persistence and feedback go hand in hand, and fostering the former means that we must furnish the latter.

Seeing Errors as Opportunities for Learning (and Celebrating Those Errors)

Let's get real. No one likes to be wrong. When was the last time you failed at doing something and cheerily reminded yourself, "Now I've got an opportunity to learn!" The failure to accomplish something can be demoralizing, especially in the absence of support. However, failure can also be productive, especially when it is followed with further instruction and feedback. Imagine if classrooms were places where errors were celebrated as opportunities to learn. Over time, we might all learn to welcome the opportunities that our errors provide us for learning.

Kapur (2016) describes four possible learning events: *unproductive failure* (unguided problem solving), *unproductive success* (memorizing an algorithm, without understanding why), *productive failure* (using prior knowledge to figure out a solution, followed by more instruction), and *productive success* (structured problem solving). Of the four conditions, unproductive failure yields the smallest gains, as students' thinking is not guided in any way, and they are just expected to discover what should be learned. Unproductive success is also of limited value, as students in this condition rely on memorization only but don't ever get to why and how this is applied. There's just no transfer of knowledge. (Nancy regrets the years she wasted in high school math under the mistaken belief that if she could just memorize the formulas, she'd somehow understand algebra. Thank goodness she finally met a math teacher who knew better.)

Now let's move to the beneficial conditions: productive failure and productive success. Kapur explains:

> The difference between productive failure and productive success is a subtle but an important one. The goal for productive failure is a preparation for learning from subsequent instruction. Thus, it does not matter if students do not achieve successful problem-solving performance initially. In contrast, the goal for productive success is to learn through a successful problem-solving activity itself. (p. 293)

Both are necessary for learning. In productive success conditions, students are guided to resolve problems (not just memorize formulas). For instance, in a close reading lesson, students approach a complex text that stretches their deep comprehension, as the teacher carefully scaffolds their understanding by posing text-dependent questions that move from literal to structural to inferential questions (Frey & Fisher, 2013). But in order for students to become assessment capable, they need to also experience productive failure. Keep in mind that these are opportunities for students to apply what they already know in an attempt to resolve a problem, with further subsequent supports available to refine their knowledge. These are small but important failures, not the soul-crushing kind that makes a student want to throw up his hands in frustration. Figure 5.4 summarizes the types of learning events and their outcomes. To extend our close reading example, students sometimes take on complex texts initially in the company of peers, even if it is initially unsuccessful. After students have had a chance to use what they know, the teacher joins them to provide further instruction.

Video 5.4
Viewing Errors
as Opportunities

*resources.corwin.com/
assessment-capable*

Video 5.5
Viewing Errors as
Opportunities in
High School Math

*resources.corwin.com/
assessment-capable*

Figure 5.4   Four Possible Learning Events

	Unproductive Failure	Unproductive Success	Productive Success	Productive Failure
Type of Learning Event	Unguided problem solving without further instruction	Rote memorization without conceptual understanding	Guided problem solving using prior knowledge and tasks planned for success	Unsuccessful or suboptimal problem solving using prior knowledge, followed by further instruction
Learning Outcome	Frustration that leads to abandoning learning	Completion of the task without understanding its purpose or relevance	Consolidation of learning through scaffolded practice	Learning from errors and ensuring learners persist in generating and exploring representations and solutions
Useful for . . .			Surface learning of new knowledge firmly anchored to prior knowledge	Deep learning and transfer of knowledge
Undermines . . .	Agency and motivation	Goal setting and willingness to seek challenge		
Promotes . . .			Skill development and concept attainment	Use of cognitive, metacognitive, and affective strategies

online resources Available for download at **resources.corwin.com/assessment-capable**

Eighth-grade English teacher Kevin Kearney distributed a short poem by Carl Sandburg (1918) called "Grass" to his students and asked them to read it and discuss its meaning. The students were familiar with the literary technique of personification, and Sandburg uses it well (see Figure 5.5).

However, even though his students could identify the literary technique, they were not able to glean the deeper meaning of the poem. While most of the groups inferred that Gettysburg might refer to the site of the largest battle of the U.S. Civil War, they were not familiar with the other places in the poem. Mr. Kearney listened as his students struggled to interpret the poem, and then sat with each to provide a bit more information. "*The other places named in the poem are battles from other wars. World War I, the Napoleonic Wars . . . each was a battle with heavy*

Figure 5.5   "Grass" by Carl Sandburg

Grass

Pile the bodies high at Austerlitz and Waterloo.

Shovel them under and let me work—

I am the grass; I cover all.

And pile them high at Gettysburg

And pile them high at Ypres and Verdun.

Shovel them under and let me work.

Two years, ten years, and passengers ask the conductor:

What place is this?

Where are we now?

I am the grass.

Let me work.

losses," he continued. *"Now that you know that, can you locate the deeper meaning of the poem and determine what is special about the grass?"* In other words, the students were experiencing productive failure, followed by short instruction on new knowledge.

Armed with additional information, the groups returned to their task. After rereading the poem a few more times, Eduardo's group was the first to arrive at the answer. They called their teacher over. *"We think it's the grass in a cemetery,"* said Eduardo. *"Tell me more,"* said Mr. Kearney. *"I'd like some elaboration, and give me some evidence."* The students glanced at one another and discussed the question before turning back to the teacher. *"Like a military cemetery, where they have all the graves of the soldiers,"* said Bethany. *"And here's our evidence,"* continued Devonte. *"He keeps saying about the bodies 'piling high' and he uses the word 'shovel' like a gravedigger would have to do."*

QUESTIONS FOR REFLECTION

How might you help students see errors as opportunities for learning?

"*I like it, I like it,*" said the teacher. "*Now go even deeper. How come those battles? What do they have in common? And how could you find that out? Put your heads together again to solve this next challenge.*" At this point in the lesson, the students were experiencing productive success because they were leveraging new concepts to deepen their understanding of the text.

What's remarkable was what the group had to say about the lesson after class was over. Bethany remarked that her teacher "gives us time to figure things out, and it's not like we have to be right all at once." Devonte added, "Mr. Kearney's always got another trick up his sleeve. Sometimes I try to figure out what the clue is going to be. I like trying to get in his head." This is a hallmark of an assessment-capable visible learner. There isn't a false expectation equating being "right" with being a "good student." Even more importantly, students recognize that wrestling for a bit with a problem is part of learning. Best yet, those like Devonte are visibly teaching themselves as they consciously examine how learning unfolds.

Conclusion

Feedback and challenge can play a reciprocal role in fueling the learning of students. The feedback opportunities we create for students should correspond to three avenues: self, peers, and teachers. Consider it this way—in an environment where students are making errors, they need to be drenched in feedback to regain momentum, think strategically, and take action. In places where feedback is nonexistent or unproductive, the learner can become paralyzed or even give up. Worst of all, she might rightly come to the conclusion that she's better off playing it safe because errors just make her feel sorry. As we noted in Chapter 1, challenge ("not too hard, not too boring") is a high-yield approach to learning. The students in Mr. Kearney's class aren't afraid of some challenge, in part because he has created the conditions that make the learning environment optimal for some academic risk taking. In the chapter that follows, we'll examine practices that he and other teachers like him utilize to ensure that students are equal participants in their own learning.

ASSESSMENT–CAPABLE VISIBLE LEARNERS...
Monitor Progress and Adjust Their Learning

CHAPTER

6

© Robin Nelson/PhotoEdit

> *"I don't know a lot about this topic, and it's making me feel a little stressed. I need to ask clarifying questions and take good notes, I have to learn it. Not my teacher."*

This was Valerie's written reflection on the question her teacher posted at the beginning of class. "How much do you know about this topic? What strategies will you need to use today to be successful?"

The students in Nicolette Adams' ninth-grade humanities class use self-questioning, individually and with peers, regularly to address course essential questions and daily lessons. It is key if they are going to monitor and adjust their learning. For this unit of study on Mexican history, culture, geography, and the arts, Ms. Adams used the essential question, "What happens when civilizations clash?" During the four weeks devoted to this unit, students examined the early dominant Mexican civilizations, the conflicts that arose during the Spanish conquest and its lasting repercussions on Mexican society and the United States. Students read *Bless Me, Ultima* (Anaya, 1994), examined pre-Columbian and contemporary Mexican art, and plotted the shifting political borders of the country during the last 400 years.

As Ms. Adams explained,

> Humanities are a big bite for students. We're incorporating many disciplines. Not just history, geography, and English, but also the arts, science, and even religion. I introduce two types of questions at the beginning of the year for them to discuss and sometimes write about each day. One set of questions is about the content we're learning. The second set is about how *they* are learning.

Ms. Adams has these questions posted in her classroom, and her students glue them to the inside cover of their journals for referencing (see Figure 6.1). She usually assigns a specific question from each column, but on some days she lets them choose the questions they will respond to.

After reviewing the learning intentions and success criteria for a lesson about the consequences of the Spanish conquest on the lives of indigenous peoples, especially because of disease, students read an excerpt from *Guns, Germs, and Steel: The Fates of Human Societies* (Diamond, 1999) on the effect of smallpox on the Aztecs, which contributed to Spanish victories. Ms. Adams asks her students to respond in writing to the question, *"How much do you know about today's topic?"* before discussing at their tables. Valerie confesses that she

Figure 6.1 Self-Questions for Content Knowledge and Learning

Questions About Content Knowledge	Questions About Your Own Learning	
	Before the Lesson	After the Lesson
• How do the mythologies, religious practices, or culture customs influence this society? • How are these concepts similar to or different from today's beliefs and values? • How did the geography of the region influence outcomes? • In what ways did people positively and negatively respond to this event? • In what ways are the ideals of the time expressed through art, music, and literature? • How did racial, ethnic, economic class, or gender differences and beliefs shape this society? • What role did technological advances play in the rise or fall of this society? • How did conflict lead to change, either positively or negatively?	• How much do you know about today's topic? • Why is this topic important? • What strategies will you need to use today to be successful? • What do you expect to be easy about today's lesson? What will be hard?	• What was most confusing for you today? • What new knowledge did you acquire in today's lesson? • What strategy worked best for you today, and why? • What do you need to know next? What wonderings do you have that I have not addressed?

online resources Available for download at **resources.corwin.com/assessment-capable**

doesn't know what smallpox is, but assumes it must be bad. Sarahi fills in a few details, explaining that *"I know it's a disease that doesn't exist anymore. I don't know what it caused, but I agree it must have been bad because there was this worldwide effort to get rid of it."* Abdulrahim perks up. *"Oh yeah, we learned about that last year in science!"* Listening to the conversation, Thomas adds, *"So if there's this bad disease that caused lots of people to die, wouldn't it be just as bad for the Spaniards?"* The group agrees, and Valerie adds Thomas's question to a list of ideas they want to explore.

After each table shares the one or two anticipatory questions they have, Ms. Adams dives into the heart of her instruction. Fifty-five minutes later, with ten minutes left before the end of the period, the teacher now poses a content knowledge question from the list. *"We've discussed several factors that played a role in Cortes's success in conquering the Aztecs, such as superior technology and the high cost of disease on the Aztecs. Please take a few minutes to address this question in your journals: What role did technological advances play in the rise or fall of this society?"*

As the students write, Ms. Adams explains:

> I can't read all of their responses every single day. I see 180 stu-
> dents a day. But I make a point of selecting five journals each
> period to review. It gives me a sense of what they're under-
> standing. But it's not just me that needs to know. Every Friday, I
> devote a longer section of the class to writing. They reread their
> self-questioning notes from the week and then respond to other
> questions about their progress toward their goals, what they still
> need, and their plan to get there. While they write, I get a chance
> to check in with more students about their learning. It took me
> awhile to realize that it's not about "covering the curriculum"
> [making air quotes with her fingers]. Go deep, and make sure
> they see their own learning.

The most effective student we know of is a self-questioning one. A
learner who can pose questions to herself and act upon the answers
is one who is virtually unstoppable. The ability to do so is one that
develops through lots of opportunities to engage in self-reflection and
self-questioning, which has an effect size of 0.64 (Hattie, 2012). There's
great value in self-questioning, as it can be the catalyst needed for monitoring one's own learning and making adjustments accordingly. The
more we can move students to active decision making about their own
learning, the more assessment capable they become.

In this chapter, we will discuss the value of self-questioning and critical
questioning among peers, especially in discussion. Questioning and discussion are rooted in developing a deeper awareness of what a learner
understands. All of us have had the experience of holding a naïve belief
in our own comprehension of a concept, only to realize that when we
tried to actually talk about it with someone else, we didn't have a good
grasp after all. That cognitive dissonance probably didn't sit well with
you, either, and you set about getting yourself up to speed. That's what
assessment-capable visible learners can do—they engage in questioning
and discussion to monitor their understanding and adjust their learning
plan as needed. They are prepared to hold conflicting ideas, see inconsistencies in their own thinking, and feel safe to explore these aloud with
their peers and teacher. The latter portion of the chapter addresses goal
setting and acting upon those goals. Student goal setting is also a powerful catalyst for learning, as students own their learning.

Reflective Self-Questioning

The ability to query one's own understanding is a metacognitive strategy that assists in a learner's ability to self-regulate. We have discussed

> The most effective
> student we know of
> is a self-questioning
> one. A learner who
> can pose questions to
> herself and act upon the
> answers is one who is
> virtually unstoppable.

metacognition and self-regulation in earlier chapters, so suffice it to say that self-questioning provides a student insight into what she knows and does not know, and how she might move forward in her learning. Self-questioning can be useful as a study skill, especially in learning new material. A valuable reading comprehension strategy is to teach students to pause and pose questions to themselves to check for understanding of what they have read. Reciprocal teaching, which we will spotlight in the next chapter, can build this habit of monitoring one's reading comprehension (Palincsar & Brown, 1984). In this chapter, however, we examine self-questioning as a means for students to gain insight into their own learning.

Self-questioning for insight and reflection is a function of curiosity. Children who see the learning they are doing as something relevant and interesting to them are likely to be inclined to ask further questions of themselves and of the topic they are studying. This is often associated with inquiry learning, although we think that term is limiting. Too often we have witnessed well-meaning educators launch into inquiry-based units of instruction, hoping to foster the kind of curiosity they long to see in their students. But curiosity and confusion are not one and the same. Without adequate foundational—surface—knowledge about the topic, students are more likely to be puzzled, and quite frankly dismissive, when they lack the background knowledge they need to actually ask reflective questions. It's nearly impossible to contrive a creative solution when you know little about what it is or why you should care. This is why problem-based learning has such a poor overall effect; it's implemented too soon in the learning cycle. With an overall effect size of 0.15, problem-based learning seems to bear little fruit (Hattie, 2012); similarly inquiry-based teaching has a low effect size. However, when problem-based learning is introduced after students have deepened their learning on a topic, the effect size rises to 0.61 (Fisher, Frey, & Hattie, 2016). We'll put it another way: You need to know a lot in order to ask solid questions, to explore inconsistencies, to inquire and problem solve. That is not to say that students must wait for self-questioning to emerge. The regular use of reflective prompts can activate the kind of questioning we want learners to use reflexively.

First-grade teacher Charlotte Bradenton has been using "I can" statements to assist her young students in monitoring their progress ("I can" statements also help students understand the success criteria). "But it took me awhile to realize I could turn these into tools for self-questioning," she said. Ms. Bradenton posts "Can I?" questions to encourage self-questioning. "Six-year-olds haven't developed the habit of self-inquiry," said the teacher, "so I help them with it." In

Video 6.1
Teaching Young Children to Monitor Their Progress

resources.corwin.com/assessment-capable

the second quarter of the school year, she introduced several "Can I?" questions for students to use:

- Can I tell the order of events in a story?

- Can I explain the charts, diagrams, or maps used in an informational book?

- Can I compare new information I read about with what I already know?

- Can I write about what I have read?

"Each time I meet with a child to discuss a reading, we go back to these four questions," the teacher explained. "These represent the major skills I am teaching right now, and I want my students to be able to apply these across lots of things they read, not just a single story. By encouraging them to ask questions of themselves, they learn to check in with their own understanding. It's not just me that's informing them that they've learned something."

Collaboration to Foster Self-Questioning

Learning is largely a social endeavor, and opportunities to hear what others are thinking as they try ideas on for size and work toward consensus can be of immense value. Participation in small group discussions can provide learners with the chance to express their own thoughts, especially as new insight is sometimes borne from the very act of trying to explain something to someone else. The effect size for students who regularly work together collaboratively and cooperatively is 0.42, in large measure because the tasks are structured to provoke interdependence upon one another. Social engagement is a foundational skill for collaborative learning, as the student's engagement with the group is essential. You will recall the self-assessment for engagement in Chapter 1 (Figure 1.1), which is a useful tool that prompts self-reflection about contributions to the group.

But there are other forces at work during collaborative learning situations. In addition to the social and emotional development of students, collaborative learning can foster critical thinking, increase cognitive engagement, and promote the use of problem solving skills (Laal & Ghodsi, 2012). Students working collaboratively in pairs or small groups must be taught to listen carefully, consider the ideas of others, present their own, and come to consensus. These are not inconsequential and are honed over a lifetime of experiences working with others. Students can, and need to, be taught these skills. Because much of the exchanges within the group are verbal, it is useful for students to possess tools for doing so. Accountable talk is one such tool (Michaels, O'Connor, & Resnick, 2008) that rests on three commitments:

- *Accountability to the learning community* is about how students talk with one another. They listen carefully and respectfully agree and disagree with one another as they resolve a problem. Students might ask, "Could you please repeat that?" or invite a team member who has not yet contributed to the discussion for his thoughts or reactions.

- *Accountability to accurate knowledge* is about the content of their discussion. Students offer evidence to support claims, and ask one another questions such as, "Can you show us where you found that information in the book?" Members of an accountable community strive to locate and share accurate information, as they understand that the performance of the group rests on it.

- *Accountability to rigorous thinking* is about the logic used by group members. Students expect to be asked about their reasoning and may be asked, "Can you tell us why you think that is an important detail?" or "I don't understand why you did that last calculation. Can you explain it?"

When students learn to routinely ask these questions of one another, the habit of self-questioning becomes part of the collaborative learning routines. Accountable talk fuels peer feedback, too. We should say that these processes do not emerge simply because four students are seated at a table. We want to distinguish collaborative learning from sharing. The personal recollections and experiences of students have some value, but on their own aren't going to result in deep learning. Sharing goals, values, and beliefs are characteristics of basic group work, but they lack the kind of accountable talk dimensions described above (Fisher & Frey, 2014). The use of the dimensions of accountable talk in collaborative learning shifts the attention to critical listening, thinking, and the use of argumentation.

QUESTIONS FOR REFLECTION

In what ways could you foster accountable talk in the classroom?

How might you use accountable talk to make collaboration more effective?

Think-Outside-the-Box Questions

The habit of self-questioning is further supported when students learn to think together and individually, both critically and creatively. To do so requires that they develop intellectual habits they can engage in with increasing automaticity, in order to foster transfer of learning. Transfer of learning is the ultimate measure of learning, as students are able to apply skills, concepts, and knowledge in increasingly new and novel situations (Hattie, Fisher, & Frey, 2016). That means they need to wrestle with rigorous questions that push their thinking. These intellectual habits can be guided through the use of questioning processes that cause students to consider what is known, seek patterns, speculate, draw conclusions, and arrive at creative solutions. Figure 6.2 features a flowchart and sample questions that can be utilized by student teams as they work through challenging texts and problems. These "think-outside-the-box" questions, adapted from the work of King (1992), are not isolated questions to be selected off a list, but rather provide the discussion group with a map of how to move their thinking forward through each stage.

Figure 6.2   Think-Outside-the-Box Questions

Clarify Understanding
What do we already know about . . . ?
Explain how . . . ?
Explain why . . . ?
What is the meaning of . . . ?

Look for Relationships
How does . . . tie in with what we learned before?
How does . . . affect . . . ?
How are . . . and . . . similar?
What is the difference between . . . and . . . ?
How does . . . cause . . . ?

Speculate
How would you use . . . to . . . ?
Compare . . . and . . . with regard to . . . .
What do you think causes . . . ?

Make Judgments
What are the strengths and weaknesses of . . . ?
Why is . . . important?
What is the best . . . and why?

Think Creatively
What is a new example of . . . ?
What would happen if . . . ?
What are some possible solutions to the problem of . . . ?

Source: Adapted from King, A. (1992). Facilitating elaborative learning through guided student-generated questioning. *Educational Psychologist, 27*(11), 111–126.

Natalya Alvarez-Gallagher has developed a version of think-outside-the-box questions to foster habits of self-questioning for her third graders. While her students are working collaboratively, solving rich mathematical tasks, Ms. Alvarez-Gallagher intermittently pauses the action to pose questions. "I call them 'think breaks' and I post a question for all of them to see," she explained. "They stop what they're doing to check in with each other, especially so they can monitor how it's going, or if they have overlooked something." These extended math tasks often take 15 minutes or so, and have lots of text and data for the students to wade through. The mathematical task these students were completing involved a challenge in developing a plan for planting a garden that would allow for the largest number of plants to be planted within a fixed area. The students would need to determine the best plan among three they had been given. They also needed to select among several choices of seeds, each of which varied in the area needed for optimal growth. At varying points throughout the time allotted for the task, the teacher would pause their thinking with a series of questions:

- **Clarify your understanding:** What do we know about this problem? What are we being asked to do? (*Question posed after a two-minute initial review of the task.*)

- **Look for relationships:** How is this problem similar to what we have been learning in math? (*Question posed four minutes into the activity.*)

- **Speculate:** What are we sure of? What mistakes should we watch out for? (*Question posed ten minutes into the activity.*)

- **Make judgments:** Is there something we can eliminate? Is there an idea that seems best? (*Question posed 12 minutes into the activity.*)

- **Think creatively:** How would our answer change if we had fewer seeds? (*Question posed at the end of the activity.*)

The teacher noted that she has seen a shift in her students' thinking as the year progressed. "I always have some students who are in a rush to solve the problem as quickly as they can, and they don't really involve the other members of the group," she said. "These questions are causing them to slow down and listen to others. It's also giving them a way to check their own thinking. I've started posting these same questions on their math assessments, too, as a reminder that math is about thinking, not being a calculator."

Science is a discipline that prizes the intellectual habit of argumentation. However, students don't readily engage in this without instruction and support. The students in sixth-grade science teacher Sylvia Romero's class use language frames on their lab days to discuss their results before composing their lab reports (see Figure 6.3). Ms. Romero introduced them at the beginning of the year as a tool for shaping their discussions. "In past years, I observed lots of trading of information in the lab groups. You know, 'What answer did you write for number 6?' It was about task completion, which I get, but not so much about learning." Ms. Romero restructured her lab report format in order to shift the focus from listing results to thinking critically about why they obtained the results they did. The introduction of argumentation language frames assisted students to engage in more self-questioning. Toby, a student in her class, explained:

> Ms. Romero has us write our own reflection before and after the lab discussion, and we have to speculate and offer counterclaims. We each developed a model for what we thought would happen to water molecules when they changed states. Like from liquid, to solid, to gas. And then I wrote my hypothesis. But when we worked in our lab groups, we had to test everyone's model and then make some decision about which model was the most accurate. Science isn't about you being right. It's about finding out what's accurate. You gotta take yourself out of the equation for the team to really get it.

The science teacher, who was listening to Toby, asked, *"And what did you discover?"* Toby said,

> Well first, it turns out that Gretchen had the best model in our group. And Bryce really helped me because he asked a question for all of us about whether the water molecules lose energy when they change states of matter. I hadn't even thought of that one. We read that it was all about the spacing between the molecules. So, in my reflection, I wrote that his speculation helped me think about a new idea.

Discussion in the classroom further promotes self-questioning and self-reflection, and with an effect size of 0.82, bears out the potential for significant learning. However, whole group discussion is not the all-too-familiar Initiate-Respond-Evaluate (IRE) model that seems to dominate classroom discourse. This phenomenon, documented by Cazden (1988) and many others, often goes like this:

Teacher: *What's the capital of the Czech Republic?* (Initiates)

Student: *Prague?* (Responds)

Teacher: *Correct!* (Evaluates)

Figure 6.3   Language Frames for Argumentation in Science

Making a Claim	I observed _____ when _____. I compared _____ and _____. I noticed _____ when _____. The effect of _____ on _____ is _____.
Providing Evidence	The evidence I use to support _____ is _____. I believe _____ (statement) because _____ (justification). I know that _____ is _____ because _____. Based on _____, I think _____. Based upon _____, my hypothesis is _____.
Asking for Evidence	I have a question about _____. Does _____ have more _____? What causes _____ to _____? Can you show me where you found the information about _____?
Offering a Counterclaim	I disagree with _____ because _____. The reason I believe _____ is _____. The facts that support my idea are _____. In my opinion, _____. One difference between my idea and yours is _____.
Inviting Speculation	I wonder what would happen if _____. I have a question about _____. Let's find out how we can test these samples for _____. We want to test _____ to find out if _____. If I change _____ (variable in experiment), then I think _____ will happen because _____. I wonder why _____? What caused _____? How would this be different if _____? What do you think will happen if _____ occurs next?
Reaching Consensus	I agree with _____ because _____. How would this be different if _____? We all have the same idea about _____.

Source: Ross, D., Fisher, D., & Frey, N. (2009). The art of argumentation. *Science and Children, 47*(3), 28–31.

While we're happy the student is learning European capitals, it should be noted that this type of exchange is not what we mean by classroom discussion. Rather, discussions are opportunities for students to explore the thinking of others, and in the process, gain insight into their own. Classroom discussions may be facilitated by the teacher or by students, but in either case capitalize on critical thinking processes similar to those featured in collaborative reasoning and reciprocal teaching (both profiled in this book), and linked to dimensions of accountable talk. Socratic seminar and debates are two examples of formal classroom discussion. However, many more discussions take place that are informal. In all cases, discussions are driven in significant ways by the students themselves, with the teacher serving as facilitator and guide rather than director.

By their nature, classroom discussions are not heavily orchestrated by the teacher. In true discussion, people listen carefully to one another and respond in the moment, without an intermediary who decides who gets to speak next. That means students need to acquire the skills of gaining and yielding the floor. We recall being in a fifth-grade classroom with a skilled teacher who would gently but firmly turn the discussion back to her students when it wandered back to her. During a discussion about colonial America's Stamp Act of 1765, a student turned to her to speak. *"Thank you, but I'm not your audience. They are,"* said the teacher as she swept her hand from left to right. *"Engage with them so that they can consider your thoughts."*

In addition to learning how to enter and exit such discussions, students need opportunities to engage in self-questioning and self-reflection. It's hard to do so when time isn't carved out for this purpose. One method is to simply pause the discussion after a short period of warming up to the topic, before entering the central portion of the discussion. Lewis Evans, a ninth-grade English teacher, "pushes the pause button," as he describes it, so that students can collect their thoughts. During a discussion of the book *The Hate U Give* (Thomas, 2017), students pondered the dilemma of Starr, the protagonist, who has witnessed a police shooting that leaves her childhood friend Khalil dead. Starr has decided not to come forward as a witness, all the while recognizing her own cultural code switching as she navigates the dualities of being an African American teen from a stressed community who attends an exclusive private school as a scholarship student.

After an opening ten-minute discussion of the varying and contentious opinions about Starr's decision, Mr. Evans asks his students to "lower the volume and listen to your own thoughts. Where are you at right now in your thinking? What two amazing questions are you going to pose to

In true discussion, people listen carefully to one another and respond in the moment, without an intermediary who decides who gets to speak next. That means students need to acquire the skills of gaining and yielding the floor.

the class when we pick up the discussion? Write all of that down on the Google Doc I set up for us."

Shortly thereafter, Mr. Evans brings the class back together and projects the questions on a screen. *"Which would you like to take on first?"* They decide that Crystal's question is one they need to discuss first. Her question reads, "Starr tells us that the title comes from Tupac's statement that Thug Life means 'The Hate U Give Little Infants F***s Everybody.' How does this influence her decision?"

The group pauses on the question, and then Antonio offers, *"Starr was thinking about how messed up things are in her community, and she didn't want to contribute any more to that."*

"Tell me what you mean when you say, 'contribute to that,'" said Jessie.

"What I mean is that there's the 'no snitch' expectation. Starr talked about it. Going to the police with info just isn't cool," Antonio explains.

"OK, I can see that, but Starr had information that would help to break the case open. That it was an unjustified police shooting," Marco counters. *"Wouldn't it have been better for her to cooperate with them?"*

"I can understand where you're going with that," Janelle replies. *"But Starr's also got the horrible memory of seeing another friend shot in a drive-by* [shooting] *when she was in elementary school. That's some PTSD* [post-traumatic stress disorder] *there."*

Crystal, the student who first proposed the question, now said, *"I'm going to call the question. 'Thug Life.' I'm interested in hearing what you all think about this as an influence on her decision. I can't help but hear that echo in my head, and I wonder if it echoed in hers."*

Lora speaks next. *"I think Tupac was commenting on the fact that racial and ethnic hatred ends up damaging us as a society."* Antonio continues, *"And gets perpetuated generation after generation."* Marco, listening closely, adds, *"So Starr's own personal experiences with racism have brought her to this point. She's feeling the conflict of obeying her instincts. Avoid the police always. But she's also feeling the internal pressure of wondering if she can't flip the script on this. It's not as easy as I'd like to believe."*

As the discussion continued, Mr. Evans takes notes on the board to collect their thoughts. "Later in the discussion, I'll have them return to these ideas and ask them to write again about their perspectives on the protagonist's decision. I want them to see the evidence of how their understanding deepens as they listen to one another." Note one of the major powers of such classroom discussions, is that teachers can "hear" their impact. They can hear what they may have taught well, what needs reteaching, who is fluent, who is struggling with ideas, and where support is needed.

Consider the Initiate-Respond-Evaluate model of class discussion.

How would a classroom look and sound differently if a teacher used accountable talk and collaboration?

Self-Questioning to Reflect on Goals

The questioning and discussion we provoke with students must include another vital element: an opportunity to reflect on goals. After all, if students are engaging in all this metacognitive thinking, but not actually applying it to figure out where they're at and where they're headed, then we will have squandered a valuable opportunity to build assessment-capable visible learners. Student goal setting should be linked to the success criteria developed for the lesson, unit, or assignment. There are two elements to consider when it comes to goals. The first is the students' goal orientation—*why* they do what they do—and the second is goal setting—*what* they do to get there (Martin, 2013). Goal orientation can be either mastery or performance. Martin explains, "Mastery orientation is focused on factors and processes such as effort, self-improvement, skill development, learning, and the task at hand. Performance orientation is focused more on demonstrating relative ability, social comparison, and outperforming others" (p. 353). In other words, it's the difference between saying "I want to learn to speak Spanish" (mastery) rather than "I want to get an A in Spanish (performance)." Although it may seem innocuous, a performance orientation often results in diminished academic risk taking and adventurousness (Martin, Marsh, & Debus, 2003). That's why we cringe when we see public displays of data that position one student against another. A chart that has everyone's reading level posted reinforces social comparisons. Instead, we want students to gain a mastery orientation, which is positively associated with effort, learning, and improvement. With just a bit of shaping, that public data chart could report on each child's gains and the number of books read, for example, rather than on the individual's current reading level.

Goal setting—what they do to get there—is the second element of the formula for helping students gauge their progress. Student goal setting has a strong effect size of 0.50 (Hattie, 2012), helping students become active participants in their own learning. The goals should be appropriately challenging (not too hard, not too boring) and should include regular check-ins so as to be motivating and to direct a student's focus and attention. It should be said that we do not subscribe to the delusionary belief that every student begins from the exact same place in his or her learning. Prior knowledge and present skill levels mean that there will be a range of starting points in every classroom. Goal setting should be about progress, not just outcomes. Seventh-grade English teacher Simon Thompson assists his students in setting and reaching reading goals. Students are assessed at the beginning of the school year to measure their current reading levels, and Mr. Thompson meets individually with each student to discuss the results. Two students stand in contrast to one another. Bianca's results were consistent with current grade-level expectations, while Cassidy's were significantly lower. Mr. Thompson began each conference by discussing the meaning of the results and then moved the conversation to current reading habits. Not surprisingly, Bianca reads more frequently than her classmate Cassidy does. To help Bianca set her goals, he focused her attention on broadening the genres and topics she was reading. He posted her goal on the class goal chart: "My goal is to read two science fiction books, a collection of poetry, and three graphic novels this quarter."

When he met with Cassidy to discuss her results, Mr. Thompson also discussed reading habits and discovered that the girl had not completed even one book the previous year. *"It sounds like that's an excellent first goal for you. I can help you choose a book you're interested in, if you want. Then we'll meet to figure out when you want to be a specific points in the book and check in with me,"* he said. He and Cassidy met again two days later, after she had chosen a book by Kwame Alexander. *"My brother showed me a video of him called* Undefeated *and I liked it, so I thought I'd check him out."* Cassidy, whose passion is basketball, chose *The Playbook: 52 Rules to Aim, Shoot, and Score in This Game Called Life* (Alexander, 2017). *"Plus, there are lots of pages that don't have lots of words on them, so I figured I could read it faster,"* she confessed. She agreed to start with the first 25 pages a week and then meet with her teacher.

By the following week, Cassidy had changed her goal. "I switched it to 35 pages 'cause I did 31 last week no sweat," she told Mr. Thompson. He changed her goal statement on the chart to reflect her new target. It now read, "I'm going to read *The Playbook*, 35 pages a week." Mr. Thompson said, *"Looks like you're going for a PR* [personal record]. *That's how you get it done."* She flipped to a page with a graphic and a large quote by Venus Williams and read it aloud to him: *"I don't focus on what I'm up against. I focus on my goal and I try to ignore the rest,"* then walked away smiling.

Planning and Organizing to Adjust Learning

Self-regulation is further evidenced as students learn to plan and make adjustments. Young children can be asked to plan for simple tasks, such as considering which materials they will need to complete an assignment, or what kinds of clothing are needed for different weather conditions. Academic planning requires a level of organization that is essential for completing more complex tasks, such as writing. Effective writers plan their writing using any number of strategies, including engaging in brainstorming to listing ideas, and freewriting to put them into motion. Freewriting is a timed writing practice used to begin to convert lists to more connected texts. When his writing stalls, ninth-grade student Kolby uses a freewriting technique he first learned in middle school. His teacher introduced him to the practice of first listing topics and ideas for a paper through a five-minute brainstorming session, followed by an additional ten minutes of freewriting. "My goal is to use as many of the words on my brainstorming list as I can, and to write at least 100 words," Kolby said. "I don't get too hung up on making sure I used all the ideas I listed, or even in whether I wrote 100 words or not," he explained. "But it definitely gets the juices flowing, and I don't have to just keep staring at a blank screen."

Fourth-grade student Jenny uses planning for her reading. "Last year my teacher taught us how to first skim a reading to look at all the headings. That gives me information about what I'm going to read about." Her classmate Israel added, "Sometimes I turn [the headings] into questions." Other planning comes in the form of thinking about the time needed. Eleventh-grade student Marcus is reading *David Copperfield* in his British literature course:

> We read *Silas Marner* last year, so I know that it takes time to work through a Dickens novel. There's like a jillion characters. We're reading it like it was originally written, in serial form. I've got Chapters 25 to 27 to read and be ready to discuss on Thursday. I put it in my calendar to block out time to read and annotate. Dude got paid by the word. Did ya know?

Jenny, Israel, and Marcus have something in common. They are not simply consuming information, but actually planning strategically for how they will understand it, especially as they confront an obstacle to their progress or anticipate a challenging task. In other words, they adjust their learning. Jenny skims and scans, Israel converts headings to questions, and Marcus uses time management and annotation in his reading. Their planning in turn serves as a way to organize their thinking, which is a second critical metacognitive skill. When we refer to organization, we don't mean the physical environment (although that is a good study skill), but rather to build schema, which is the mental structure you use to frame a network of related knowledge. For example, when you read about Marcus's assignment to read *David Copperfield*, it may have triggered elements of your own schema. *What do I know about Charles Dickens? Do I know why this was his favorite novel? What do I know about mid-nineteenth century life? What do I know about newspaper serials of the time? What experiences have I had in wading through a really long book?* The fact that you can retrieve this information speaks to your mental organization of all of this related information. It also reflects your ability to self-question, monitor, and adjust your learning as needed. That's one reason note-taking guides and concept maps can be so useful for building schema. They foster mental organization of information into categories so that the learner can retrieve it more ably. Marcus's use of annotation is a great study skill precisely because it assists the learner in organizing information to build schema.

Note-Taking

Note-taking is a powerful study skill for older students—when used correctly. That is, the purpose for taking notes is not to copy down information, but rather as a study aid to monitor one's learning. Cornell notes were first developed by William Pauk (1962), the head of the study center at Cornell University, to support law students preparing for the bar exam. He devised an ingenious way for students to record information so they could use their notes for studying. The page is divided into three sections (see Figure 6.4). The major column is on the left, a minor column on the right, and space at the bottom across the two columns. Students take notes in the major column during the lecture but do not use the other two until they are ready to study. When they study their notes, they list key ideas in the minor column on the left and then summarize their notes at the bottom of the page.

Fifth-grade teacher Michelle Hampton used Cornell notes during a unit on the water cycle. The students watched a short video, and the teacher asked her students to take notes in the major column during the video to encourage active involvement. After class discussion on the topic of the video, the teacher asked her students to work in collaborative groups to develop cues to go into the minor column on the left. These are phrased in the form of questions, as the purpose is to be able to later cover the notes while answering the questions. Micah's group developed and wrote the following:

- What is the water cycle?

- What are the four phases of the water cycle?

- What does the water cycle explain?

Figure 6.4   Cornell Notes Format

CUES	NOTES
For main ideas	• *Record lecture notes here during class.*
Can be phrased as questions	• *Use meaningful abbreviations and symbols.*
	• *Leave space to add additional information.*
Written within 24 hours after class	

SUMMARY

Main ideas and major points are recorded here.

These are written during later review sessions.

Source: Adapted from Pauk, W., & Owens, R. J. Q. (2011). *How to study in college.* Boston, MA: Wadsworth Cengage Learning.

The following day, Ms. Hampton begins the class by asking students to spend a few minutes reviewing their notes. After rereading what they have written, they cover the right column and quiz each other using the questions they recorded in the left column. After reviewing the information with one another, the teacher asks her students to turn their attention to the summary section at the bottom of their notes. *"Take a few minutes and write the most important ideas about the water cycle. This is a summary, so don't try to rewrite all the details in your notes. But think to yourself: 'What do I really need to know about this?'"* The teacher explains,

> I have to build in time for them to get good at this. It's not like they'll just wake up one day and magically know how to study. But I want them to see that we study regularly, and in manageable amounts of time, so we're totally prepared by the end of the unit.

Cornell notes are an excellent study tool, but Ms. Hampton takes it a step further because she wants her students to build the habit of monitoring their learning and adjusting accordingly. After they have composed their summaries at the bottom of the note page, they talk again with a partner. Each child rates his or her ability to explain the information from yesterday's class, using the cues as a guide. Micah tells Shelby, *"I gave myself a 2 out of 4 stars on being able to say what the water cycle explains. I was good at naming the phases, so I gave myself 4 stars for that. But I had to look at my notes to answer that third cue."* Shelby listens and replies, *"What is your plan to learn it?"* Micah thinks for a moment and says, *"I guess I don't know it as much as I should. Even when I looked at my notes, I didn't have a good answer that I could understand. So I'm gonna ask the teacher to explain it again, and I have to ask good questions so I understand it better."*

Self-regulation, planning, and organizing can help students become assessment-capable learners.

How do you envision creating these opportunities in your classroom?

Conclusion

The path to building an assessment-capable visible learner must include opportunities for students to engage in reflective self-questioning, and by extension to do so with peers. Teachers can create these opportunities, and thereby build habits, for learners to reflect on their learning. Habits such as these invite students into the act of monitoring their own progress. Unfortunately, too many students are lulled into passivity because they have learned to rely on the teacher, and not themselves, to gauge their progress. The codevelopment of mastery goals shifts the responsibility of learning, as students are invited to take charge. If this sounds a bit like student empowerment, you're correct. Assessment-capable visible learners are empowered learners.

ASSESSMENT–CAPABLE VISIBLE LEARNERS...
Recognize Their Learning and Teach Others

© Bob Daemmrich/PhotoEdit

"I've got one more skill to get for this level, and then I'll be ready for the next challenge."

Gabriela could be talking about an online game, but in fact she's discussing her computer coding skills. The seventh grader selected learning to code as the way she wanted to use her makerspace time. For 90 minutes each week, students at her middle school engage in a variety of self-directed explorations. Some of her classmates meet up in the makerspace that is set up in the school cafeteria, where large tables are filled with equipment, tools, batteries, cardboard, plastic tubing, and more than a few digital devices. Some of the students in there are tinkering, while others have a clear project in mind. Gabriela wants to experiment with robotics but discovered that she didn't have the skills and knowledge she needed to create an idea she had. "I read *Rosie Revere, Engineer* (Beaty, 2013) to my little sister, and I want to make a little robot for her that carries her crayons," she said. "First, I figured out that I needed to know how to use the 3-D printer, because I have to make some parts," she said, waving a sketch to show her idea. "But then I had to know some coding, like how to make it move." Gabriela, with assistance from her teacher, found an online tutorial to learn the basics of coding. "So I already did Sequences, Variables, and Loops, and next I'm doing Conditionals," she explained. She then glanced at the time on her smartphone. "I gotta go, though. Not much time left today and I wanna get this done."

Gabriela is an assessment-capable visible learner. She has a clear sense of where she is in her learning process, where to get help and feedback, and where she is headed. The clear and linear nature of the online program is designed to give feedback and indicate when she has successfully completed a skill. As educators, we can replicate similar processes in face-to-face as well as in online environments. In fact, it is likely you have experienced this. Perhaps you were in a scouting program and progressed through requirements for badges. Or you may have played a sport, starting first with mastering the basics before moving on to more technically challenging skills. Or you may have just decided on your own to learn something, found some resources, and put your mind to it. (Nancy's seven-year-old granddaughter and her dad are systematically working their way through a knot-tying book at the moment.)

An element each of these examples has in common is that the learner has a sense of what comes next, whether it is turning the page to the next badge, moving to the next item on the checklist, or successfully completing an online module. They know when they have learned something. A second element held in common is that there is some kind of assessment signaling your success. You may have performed a skill for a coach, taken a quiz, or tied the knot so that it looked like the one in the book. The first portion of this chapter is all about assessment. But before you groan, understand that the kinds of assessments we're talking about are specifically targeted to inform the learner. After all, how could we write about assessment-capable visible learners without devoting lots of space to assessment? In the second part of the chapter, we discuss another indicator, which is the ability to teach others. A crucial measure is that your students are clear that "the standard of knowing is *the ability to explain to others*, not *understanding when explained by others*" (Willingham, 2003). We examine the importance of peer learning and constructing opportunities where students get to teach one another about what they know.

Formative Evaluations That Inform Students

The practice of formative evaluation with students has been shown to be of benefit to teachers in making decisions about next steps in teaching, as measured by gains in student learning. With an effect size of 0.90, it is worthy of our attention (Hattie, 2012). However, the power of formative evaluation doesn't reside in the act of administering the quiz, test, or assignment. All of its power lies in (1) whether the student and the teacher understand the results, and (2) whether the teacher and the student use the results to take action on future teaching and learning. The effects of formative evaluation are amplified when students are part of the equation. In other words, formative evaluation shouldn't be done only so the teacher can make decisions (even though that's important) but also so the student can make decisions. These outcomes should be linked such that students can directly benefit from the formative evaluation that occurs, and so that the instructional decision making of teachers is transparent to students (Sztajn, Confrey, Wilson, & Edgington, 2012). That's why the clarity and understanding of the reports is so essential to the process. If the student doesn't understand what the report means, he or she can't benefit or take action. Watch a child play a video game and you'll see what we mean. How does she know whether she has made the right move or not? There are clear signals that provide feedback to her about her decision. Because she understands it, she can adjust her technique and try a different move.

> Formative evaluation shouldn't be done only so the teacher can make decisions (even though that's important) but also so the student can make decisions.

An underutilized method for implementing formative evaluation is practice testing, in which students take short quizzes to understand their command of the subject or topic. These formative practice tests are low stake and not part of the student's grade, as the emphasis here is on practice to gain self-knowledge of learning gaps. A meta-analysis of the effectiveness of formative practice testing on advancing student learning reported these findings (Adesope, Trevisan, & Sundararajan, 2017):

- Lots of practice tests didn't increase student learning. Once is often enough.

- Feedback paired with the practice test enhances learning.

- The usefulness of practice tests was strong at both the elementary and secondary levels.

- The value of formative practice tests is in students reflecting on their results.

Video 7.1

Assessments Designed to Inform Learners

resources.corwin.com/ assessment-capable

Formative practice evaluation is not confined to administration of paper-and-pencil or online quizzes. Classroom audience response systems are another form and have the added benefit of providing instant results. Sixth-grade English teacher Ivan Millan uses an audience response system that allows him to scan student responses on his tablet and display the results. His students have been reading *Among the Hidden* (Haddix, 2000), about an unnamed future society where food shortages and drought have led to a government decree that families cannot have more than two children. Luke, a third child, must be hidden away so that he will not be captured by the Population Police. Mr. Millan poses comprehension questions for his students to respond to, so that they can gauge their understanding of the book. After taking a five-question audience response quiz about three-quarters of the way through the novel, the students in his class analyzed their results and met in teams aligned to the questions. Ana did not answer two of the questions correctly but was especially puzzled by the fourth question, which asked about an historical allusion to American Revolutionary War patriot Patrick Henry's statement, "Give me liberty or give me death." Ana chose to meet with a group of students who had selected the same question so that they could build each other's knowledge. Ana and several other students did an internet search of the quote and read the background information about it. *"Oh, I remember this now!"* she said. *"We learned about him [Patrick Henry] last year in social studies, right?"* Ana and the others reaffirmed their background knowledge and tied Henry's act to the protest the children in the novel were planning. Ana later remarked, "When I read that Luke 'found it in an old book' it went right past me. I like the quizzes he [Mr. Millan] gives because it helps me see things I didn't notice the first time. I'm reading Chapters 23 and 24 tonight, so I'll look for things about being a patriot."

Interpreting Their Data

Students own their own data (Hattie, 2009), and as such, students should be the consumers of their performance results, not just the teacher. However in practice, that is not always the case, even with the advent of digital grade books which make it much easier for students to see their own progress. Individual data about progress toward goals not only assists students in making strategic decisions about current learning but can also signal to them when they are ready for the next challenge. Some of the simplest ways to do so are to have students keep physical or digital data logs that can display results in graph or chart form. For young children, keeping track of their progress on graph paper can help them with their planning. For instance, we use graph paper for students to see what they have accomplished on timed writing events such as power writing (Fisher & Frey, 2007). Students write in three one-minute rounds to build writing fluency and then reread what they have written. They circle errors in spelling, grammar, or content (a self-assessment in itself), and count the number of words written each round. The highest number of words is graphed and kept in their writing folders. Thus, each student is able to see his own progress over an extended period of time as he becomes a more fluent writer.

Kindergarten teacher Wendy Sun gave each student in her class a reading data folder for the first semester of the year so that they could see goals, track progress, and make decisions about new challenges. Students keep track of their accomplishments using a variety of stickers and stamps, and their teacher uses the folder with them for conferencing. "I give them this data sheet so they can see when they are ready for a new one," said the teacher (see Figure 7.1). Ms. Sun's student Noah was busy stamping his own data sheet while his teacher was explaining it. "Here's how it works," said Noah. "When I get all the stamps, I can get a new one. I have [counting] 1, 2, 3, 4 . . . four more books to read. An' I still need to be able to write two more words 'fore a get a new one." Ms. Sun smiled and said, "I started using these last year when our school moved to student-directed family conferences. It's great to hear the kids explain to their families what they have accomplished and where they're headed next."

Public data displays can be useful, provided trust has been built and progress has been emphasized. These "status of the class" displays can track the number of students who are attaining milestones. In some schools, teachers track reading goal progress, not performance, using colored dots. The data include the number of books read. Students can then compare their own efforts to those of classmates. Seventh-grade student Jake looked at the board and said that he could see he wasn't

> Students own their own data (Hattie, 2009), and as such, students should be the consumers of their performance results, not just the teacher.

Figure 7.1   Kindergarten Student Reading Chart

I can name the capital letters of the alphabet.

A	B	C	D	E	F	G	H	I	J	K	L	M

N	O	P	Q	R	S	T	U	V	W	X	Y	Z

I can name the lowercase letters of the alphabet.

a	b	c	d	e	f	g	h	i	j	k	l	m

n	o	p	q	r	s	t	u	v	w	x	y	z

I can write my first name. _____

I can write my last name. _____

This is how many words I can write on my own:

1.	6.	11.
2.	7.	12.
3.	8.	13.
4.	9.	14.
5.	10.	15.

This is how many books I have read:

1.	6.	11.	16.	21.
2.	7.	12.	17.	22.
3.	8.	13.	18.	23.
4.	9.	14.	19.	24.
5.	10.	15.	20.	25.

Now I'm ready for a new challenge!

[online resources] Available for download at **resources.corwin.com/assessment-capable**

spending as much time reading as others in his class. "I only got one book read this quarter. There's only a couple of dots for 1–3 books. Most of the dots are for 4–6 books." He shifted over to a second chart tracking growth toward goals. "I looked at mine this morning with my teacher, and I'm at 10% of my reading goal. But there are lots of dots for 30%–35% of goals. I gotta step it up."

Older students can similarly track their progress on other skills and accomplishments. Some learning management systems and electronic grade books offer statistics on scores relative to the class. A student knowing, for example, that he scored in the lowest 20% of the class on the last science competency provides more information to him than knowing that he got a grade of C. While the latter represents an average performance in terms of the criteria for the test, the former also provides information about his performance relative to the class. We are not advocating for grading on a curve or publicly displaying this information, but rather in signaling to the student that his perception of "average" may be limited, given that 80% of the class outperformed him. These class learning analytics are underutilized but offer potential for helping students understand their next steps. In most learning management programs, the analytics need to be activated by the teacher. However, this also allows the teacher to build students' capabilities for interpreting the data and planning next steps in their learning.

As noted in every chapter, students don't simply show up knowing how to be assessment capable. Their ability to do so is fostered by teachers who seek to build their capacity to be "leaders of their own learning" (Berger, Rugen, & Woodfin, 2014). In the next section, we will turn our attention to the pedagogical skills of teachers to realize the goal of producing clear-eyed learners who know when they've learned something and are ready to take their next steps.

How might you incorporate formative practice testing?

How could you use the data that you gather?

Student-Led Assessments

Student self-assessments are realized in a variety of forms throughout this book because the ability to self-assess is such a powerful engine for learning. It confirms for students what they have learned. Even better news is that teachers can equip students with tools to determine their own learning. In a previous chapter, we discussed the value of a rubric for students to use as they provide feedback to each other, where third graders gauged each other's progress on the development of a mystery. Rubrics can also be used for students to self-assess. For instance, Marc Anthony asks his middle school science students to examine their individual projects against a rubric, highlight the levels they believe they have attained, and then attach their self-assessment to the project. This practice can be quite useful for promoting self-assessment, helping students identify what they have learned so that they can teach others, and also recognize future learning needs.

Alternatively, self-assessments can come in the form of a series of questions that prompt students to evaluate their learning. Business marketing teacher James Cotton introduced what he called quality assurance questions to his high school Career and Technical Education students at the beginning of their first course. "We learned about the Deming process for quality assurance," explained Diana, one of the students in the program. "Plan, do, study, act." Pointing to a large poster on the wall, Diana read her teacher's quality assurance questions:

- **Plan**: Do I have a clear purpose and objectives?

- **Do**: Have I developed a sequence of steps to follow? Have I included testing points to see if this is meeting my objectives?

- **Study**: What are the possible causes of the problems I identify through testing?

- **Act**: Am I revising my plan and taking action until I am successful?

Diana explained that her team was developing a new yearbook product for sale at their school and that she is the project manager. She said,

> We developed a plan and set up steps, like surveying students about price points, features they wanted, and items they could do without. Then we had to meet with the yearbook staff to share our survey results. But then, there were some problems. They had all these questions—like we didn't break down the data, so we couldn't tell them about responses by grade level. So then we had to go into "study" mode. The yearbook staff was our test, and we didn't succeed.

Diana's team revised their plan, meeting with the yearbook editor and the advisor to determine what they needed to learn and then redesigned the survey. "Today in class, we're crunching the numbers and then we'll schedule another time to meet [with the yearbook editor]. That's our next step before we can go forward," said Diana. "But here's the weird thing. I've just sort of figured out it works for lots of projects, not just here," she said. "I've got Geometry homework tonight, and I'll be doing the same thing to get it done. That Deming guy was pretty smart."

Confidence ratings are another means for students to self-assess. Young children can use a "fist-to-five" method (anything from a closed hand to all five fingers displayed) to indicate their perceived success at the completion of a task, such as their knowledge level about something they have recently learned. Second-grade teacher Leona Simons introduced this method to her students at the beginning of the year. "I'd teach them some content and then do a check-in," she said. "Like we'd be learning about supply and demand in social studies, and I would ask them to hold a hand close to their chest so just I could see it. They would rank themselves from a fist [no understanding] to five fingers [very confident] about their ability to explain the difference between the two." The teacher said that by the end of the first quarter, most of her students were doing it without prompting. "Here's an example. I met with Kendrick this morning about his reading. He had selected a title that seemed a bit of a stretch for him. My face must have looked a little doubtful, because he said, 'It's a five for me, Ms. Simons. I already know a lot about taking care of dogs [the subject of the book]. My mom said we can get one after I learn more about how to take care of a dog. I think I can read this, and I know what to do if it's too hard.'" The teacher smiled and shrugged. "How can I argue with that?" she said.

Comparative Self-Assessments

Success criteria are vital for students to understand where they are going; but they can also be used to help learners recognize where to go to next. Durable success criteria that span the semester or school year lend themselves well for fostering comparative self-assessments of learning. These are rubrics and checklists that transcend a single unit or topic of study, and contain quality indicators that are applicable across similar tasks. Among the most common are writing rubrics and checklists for text types: narrative, informative, and argumentative. Ferlazzo (2010) uses comparative self-assessments with his ninth-grade students as they analyze an essay from earlier in the year to one written at the end of the year. After scoring themselves retrospectively, he asks four questions:

- Look at the scores you gave yourself on both essays. Overall, which essay was your strongest? Why?

- Look at the scores on your strongest essay. What did you do well?

- Look at the scores on your other essay. What are three things you need to get better at next year?

- In what areas of your writing would you like next year's English teacher to help you with?

Inspired by this approach, tenth-grade English teacher Salma Quezada asked her students to revisit and compare the first essay of the school year they had written with one written nine weeks later. Using a format similar to Ferlazzo's, she constructed a checklist inspired by the Smarter Balanced argumentative performance task writing rubric for Grades 6 to 11. Her students are familiar with the rubric, having used it for several years in the English classes at their school (see Figure 7.2).

Her students wrote a short reflective piece inspired by questions about where they saw their greatest area of growth, and what they targeted for further improvement. The teacher also asked each student to link strategies that had been successful for him or her to a plan for improvement. David wrote the following:

> The place I improved the most was on citations and attributions. They were messed up! But I started using the style manual to get them right. The place I need to improve is on keeping my claim tight all the way through my paper. I can see how I wandered. What worked for me on citations was checking a reference. To make my claim tighter, I need to have someone else read my drafts to see if I'm carrying it through. Like, a human reference instead of a book one.

Comparative self-assessments can create the conditions for students to reach for their own "personal bests." As with athletes who track their

Figure 7.2   Comparative Self-Assessment for Argumentative Writing

Title and Date of First Essay:	Title and Date of Second Essay:

Organization/Purpose

Claim is introduced, clearly communicated, and maintained	Claim is introduced, clearly communicated, and maintained
4 3 2 1	4 3 2 1

Transitions used to clarify relationships among ideas	Transitions used to clarify relationships among ideas
4 3 2 1	4 3 2 1

Effective introduction and conclusion	Effective introduction and conclusion
4 3 2 1	4 3 2 1

Logical progression of ideas from beginning to end	Logical progression of ideas from beginning to end
4 3 2 1	4 3 2 1

Opposing arguments clearly addressed	Opposing arguments clearly addressed
4 3 2 1	4 3 2 1

Evidence/Elaboration

Comprehensive evidence from source material integrated throughout	Comprehensive evidence from source material integrated throughout
4 3 2 1	4 3 2 1

Clear citations or attributions	Clear citations or attributions
4 3 2 1	4 3 2 1

Effective use of elaborative techniques (personal experiences)	Effective use of elaborative techniques (personal experiences)
4 3 2 1	4 3 2 1

Vocabulary appropriate for audience and purpose	Vocabulary appropriate for audience and purpose
4 3 2 1	4 3 2 1

Effective and appropriate style enhances content	Effective and appropriate style enhances content
4 3 2 1	4 3 2 1

Conventions

Adequate use of correct sentence formation, punctuation, capitalization, grammar use, and spelling	Adequate use of correct sentence formation, punctuation, capitalization, grammar use, and spelling
4 3 2 1	4 3 2 1

online resources ⬚   Available for download at **resources.corwin.com/assessment-capable** own personal records, not just wins, learners should be encouraged to strive for new levels of attainment. As we noted in Chapter 5, our role as teachers is not just to help our students set and meet goals but to exceed their own expectations of themselves. Martin (2006) suggests that personal bests are most effective when they meet four conditions:

- Specific in nature
- Challenging to the student
- Competitively self-referenced
- Based on self-improvement

First-grade teacher Darius Morris uses personal bests with his students as they build their sight word recognition. His students compete with themselves each day in, using flash cards with high frequency words written on them. Students sort the words into piles of known and unknown words while the timer counts down 60 seconds. Students track their own performance each day, and Mr. Morris always asks, "*Who's PR'd today?*" to recognize when personal records have been attained. When Juan Carlos raised his hand and said, "*I did 45 today, my best one ever,*" the class cheered for him.

The practice of tracking personal bests works with older students, too. Middle school counselor Jim O'Neill uses personal bests to assist students at his school who struggle with regular attendance. "I work with the student and his or her family to set attendance goals, and then we track them. For some of my students, it's the realization that they are developing more stamina as they string together longer periods of consistent attendance." High school graduation coach Monique Lewis uses academic personal best approaches with students as they track their grade point averages (GPAs) and course completion records. "Some of them have low GPAs and aren't sure they can dig their way out," she said. "We set goals, track progress together, and then set new goals each time they reach a new level of personal bests," she explained. "I've been amazed at what many of them have accomplished just by keeping track of their own gains. It shifts their attention away from competing with others, and redirects their attention where it should be—demanding the best of themselves."

Self-Grading

One assessment practice commonly used in classrooms is to have students grade each other's work. There are practical benefits to this in terms of time management, but there is also the belief that learning occurs through a peer evaluation process. Of course, there are confidentiality challenges with this practice and the potential for students to tease others who do not do well. Students have to be taught how to provide feedback that is growth producing and the classroom climate needs to crafted such that errors are celebrated and are not a source of shame.

Less common is self-grading, where a student evaluates his or her own performance. But, there can be great value in self-grading assignments and tasks, with the benefit being primarily to move learning forward and signal to them what steps they need to take next. The third-grade students in Chapter 2 who self-graded their spelling words are one such example. Sadler and Good (2006) examined self-grading and peer grading in middle school classrooms. When peer grading, the identity of the learner was blinded so as not to socially influence the peer grader. Importantly, the students had been taught how to grade using rubrics—that's a critical point. Rubrics are of tremendous value when used properly—up front at the beginning of the task—because well-constructed ones provide a clear map of the success criteria. They become all the more useful when further applied in peer and self-assessment. (However, they are virtually useless when distributed for the first time just before the assessment.) The teacher also independently graded their work, checking for accuracy and offering further feedback. The researchers discovered that the grades students awarded themselves and others were reasonably aligned to the teacher's evaluation, suggesting that these learners had a good grasp of the success criteria. But on unannounced follow-up tests, the students who graded their own work outperformed those who had done the peer grading process. Why? The researchers speculate that while the metacognitive benefit of peer and self-grading was strong, the act of examining one's own work offered deeper insight and allowed the learner to make better decisions about their next steps. In the words of one seventh grader quoted in the study, "This felt strange at first . . . but by the end . . . I realized grading was another way of learning" (p. 25).

Fourth-grade student Ernesto is in a classroom that regularly employs self-grading. He explained that "the teacher still checks, so it's not like you can just give yourself an A" but has noticed the benefits in his own learning. "We had math word problems last week and we had to get the answer and explain the reasoning we used," he said. "But when I [graded] my own [paper], I had to give myself a 2 [on a 4-point rubric] for some of my answers because I didn't always have some good math reasoning." He showed one example. "See I had the right answer [pointing to the paper] but this problem was asking for me to prove it and use reasoning. I drew a model with little cubes to show how it could work, but it was for only the beginning of the problem. It wasn't

> Students have to be taught how to provide feedback that is growth producing and the classroom climate needs to crafted such that errors are celebrated and are not a source of shame.

all the way through. It was just where I started." When asked how this had impacted his thinking, he paused for a few moments and then said, "Well, I know I need to check to see if I can explain it through to the end of the problem, not just the place I start." Ernesto's teacher, Janine French, added, "When I graded his paper after he did, I saw the same omission he did. So I added feedback about the processes he was using to continue his thinking all the way through to the end of the problem."

What benefits do you envision in your classroom if your students use self-assessment and self-grading?

What concerns do you have and how might you mitigate them?

Skillful Use of Formative and Summative Evaluation

Formative and summative evaluation play an essential role in signaling learning progress to students, especially when they are actively engaged in viewing data, making strategic decisions, and taking action on next steps. These formative and summative evaluations take a variety of forms, and include both qualitative values such as rubrics, as well as quantitative measures that yield numbers. There are a number of ways to check for understanding, such as exit slips, student-led conferences, practice quizzes, story retellings, projects, and oral responses to questions (Fisher & Frey, 2015). But if students are not made a part of the formative evaluation process, learning potential goes unrealized. Eleventh-grade English teacher Kaila Tricaso ensures that her students are wholly involved in making decisions about when they have learned something and what their next steps will be simply by adding an extra question to class assignments. After reviewing the success criteria, students submit assignments and exit tickets in one of four categories:

1. I'm just learning. (I need more help.)

2. I'm almost there. (I need more practice.)

3. I own it! (I can work independently.)

4. I'm a pro! (I can teach others.)

Ms. Tricaso's formative evaluation system signals to her students that just knowing something isn't enough—the true pinnacle is when you can teach others. While not all of her students reach this stage each and every time, they have a goal in mind that is outside of self. They understand that the standard for knowing, in the words of Willingham (2003), is to be able to teach others. In addition, this simple progression causes students to gauge their own progress, identifying for themselves what the next step should be. Next steps are not always about advancing to a new topic. More often, they are about how the learner takes the next steps toward mastery.

Competency-Based Grading

Most teachers will tell you that grades are given to reflect a student's mastery of a concept or subject, but upon looking deeper, you discover that several other nonacademic factors are in the formula. Let's take a fictional student and call him Bob. Did he bring materials to class? Check. Did he turn in his homework? Sometimes. Did he behave reasonably well in class? Nope. So what's his grade for the course? Naturally, you would say that this isn't enough information and you need to know what his summative evaluations looked like. Yet too often organization, compliance, and behavior are lumped in with evaluations of learning. This is not to say that these nonacademic indicators are unimportant, but rather that when factored in with learning performance, they obscure the signal. And in this model, things quickly turn personal and undermine the relationship between the teacher and the learner. Instead of being able to tie his academic performance to his World History grade, Bob grumbles, "My teacher doesn't like me. He's always on my case. That's why I'm failing." The resentment builds, Bob only gets more sullen, and now his teacher really doesn't like him. Bob's learning trajectory looks increasingly dismal, and in the meantime, he continues to externalize as he blames others.

In an effort to end negative and ultimately futile cycles like this, more schools are turning to competency-based grading systems. This system focuses on mastery of content and eliminates grading of practice work and nonacademic behaviors. Health Sciences High has employed this system for 10 years (Fisher, Frey, & Pumpian, 2011). Students receive grades based on their performance on summative evaluations only, typically between four and six per quarter. In-class assignments and homework are regarded as formative evaluation for both the teacher and the student and do not earn points toward the course grade. Of course, some students don't do the homework (they are teenagers). However, in time, most learn the value of the practice that allows them to master the content.

Students are required to pass each summative evaluation (usually a test, essay, or other complex performance task) at a level of 70% or higher. Students who do not meet this threshold receive an Incomplete, signaling to them and their family that mastery has not yet been attained. These learners attend tutorials offered at lunchtime and after school and must complete the homework packet (whether for the first time or again) before taking another version of the exam. A decade of observation of a few thousand middle and high school students has led us to these conclusions:

- With time, most students learn the value of their active participation in their learning.

- Relationships between teachers and students are healthier because much of the subjective nature of grading has been removed.

- It's hard to initiate the change to competency-based grading and requires revisiting these policies regularly to revise and improve them.

Among the changes we have made over the years, we include adding a separate but robust citizenship grade that accompanies each academic grade, strengthening midterms and finals to include cumulative knowledge for the semester, and improving family conferences to marshal supports from home as well as school. Students who carry any Incompletes at the end of the school year are now confronted with them in summer school. Rather than offer six-week credit recovery courses, it's the Incompletes that must be addressed. Therefore, summer school may take four days for some students and longer for others. Historically, we seem to have more summer school Incompletes with younger students compared to older ones, which may be an indication of developing self-regulatory skills. By no means do we suggest that in practice a competency-based grading system is clean and easy. It's messy and hard. But we hope that our students gain a deeper understanding of themselves as learners, and what they need to do next to be successful.

Peer Learning

Assessment-capable visible learners understand that they have tools at their disposal to progress in their learning; among the most important resources they have are the peers around them. Learning is often a social act, as we learn in the company of other humans. Even in digital spaces, virtual contact with others is vital. The opportunity to speak or write can serve as a means to clarify one's own thinking about a topic. How often have you experienced a heightened sense of your own knowledge

> Among the changes we have made over the years, we include adding a separate but robust citizenship grade that accompanies each academic grade.

even as you were in the process of explaining it to someone else? This restructuring of one's own thinking is called *cognitive elaboration* and results when learners explain ideas to each other and discuss any gaps in their understanding (Chi, 2000).

The learning conditions in the classroom need to be set such that peer consultations can occur. Pausing lessons so that students can check in with one another can build the habit of conferring with others. These can range from partner checks (*"Take a moment and check with your partner to see if you both have the correct materials you'll need for this project."*) to more extended peer consultations. Our math colleague Joseph Assof uses a process called Peer-Assisted Reflection (PAR; Reinholz, 2015) with his high school students. The premise of PAR is based on the differences between novices and mathematicians in approaching difficult problems. While novices hastily identify one tool and then use it exclusively until the bitter end of the calculations, mathematicians use iterative processes that include analyzing, exploring, planning, implementing, and verifying (Schoenfeld, 1992). Students in Mr. Assof's classes complete one identified homework problem as a PAR problem, which requires that students write their reasoning as well as the calculations and solution. Students exchange the PAR problem with a partner the following day. Each partner examines the work the peer completed and annotates feedback about processes or solutions. This process typically takes about 10 minutes, at which point the students receive their original paper back, now annotated with new ideas. The teams then discuss the feedback, and then make any corrections needed before submitting it. "This is what we mean by mathematical thinking," explained Mr. Assof. "Students appreciate seeing how other classmates solved the same problem, sometimes using different processes. It gets them thinking about how they can think more flexibly, and what benefit there is to talking with others."

> Learning is often a social act, as we learn in the company of other humans. Even in digital spaces, virtual contact with others is vital. The opportunity to speak or write can serve as a means to clarify one's own thinking about a topic.

Teaching Each Other With Student Think-Alouds

Think-alouds have been used by teachers for decades to model reading comprehension strategies for their students (Davey, 1983). The purpose of a think-aloud is to voice the internal cognitive and metacognitive decisions one is making during the act of reading a passage. Fourth-grade science teacher Isabelle Franklin uses a passage from the science textbook about the differing layers of a canyon's walls, which provide evidence of a geological record over millions of years. She thinks aloud about what she is reading, and how this triggers a decision on her part:

> So as I'm reading this paragraph, I'm getting the urge to put this down in my science journal. There are two things that are

nudging me. The first is that I can see that this is an important concept. There's lots of clues, like the title of the passage and the photograph that supports it. The second thing that's nudging me is that there's lots of descriptive information here about the layers. I want a picture, but there isn't a diagram in the book. So I'm deciding to take a pause here and draw a diagram of my own in my notebook. I don't need to be a great artist. But I do need to get the layers labeled in the correct order. I've learned from experience that when I take the time to draw something like this out in my notebook, I remember the information better.

Ms. Franklin's think-aloud included why she was choosing to record her notes in this fashion. That is an item that we quite frankly often forget to share with students. Ms. Franklin creates opportunities for them to try on their own expert thinking as well, knowing that this is a mechanism for helping students become aware of their own learning, especially in the process of teaching another peer. She uses student think-alouds (Baumann, Jones, & Seifert-Kessell, 1993) to promote transfer about the learning decisions her students need to make. *"It's more than plug n' chug,"* she reminds them. *"Scholars like you know why you're doing something."* Ms. Franklin keeps a checklist for student think-alouds posted in her classroom (see Figure 7.3). She posts a question for her students and asks them to think aloud with their partner as they consider what they know and why. *"Are the top layers of a canyon's wall the youngest or the oldest? How do you know?"* Bethany and Sam watch a 90-second video on the layers of the Grand Canyon a few times and then Bethany begins:

> The narrator said that the sides of a canyon are like a book, and that each of the layers is like chapters in the book. He never said if the top of the rim was the youngest or the oldest. But he said something about the top layers being there before the ancient sea came in. Since he said "before" I think that means that they would be the youngest.

Sam continues:

> I think so, too. I was thinking about what we learned about how water cut through the rock layers. So the top would be the youngest and the bottom would be the oldest. It wasn't in the video, but it was something we read before. I'm thinking about that information when I'm listening to him.

By modeling expert decision making and creating opportunities for students to explain their own learning, they become more adept and assured of their ability to choose strategies and become cognizant of their learning.

Figure 7.3   Student Think-Aloud Checklist

☐ Let your listener(s) read through the entire question or text before you begin your think-aloud.

☐ Use "I" statements.

☐ Explain why you think you are correct, or how you know you are.

☐ Speak loudly enough for your partner(s) to hear.

☐ Don't go too fast or too slow.

☐ Make sure your think-aloud doesn't go on for more than five minutes.

Source: Fisher, D., Frey, N., & Hattie, J. (2017). *Teaching literacy in the visible learning classroom, grades K–5.* Thousand Oaks, CA: Corwin.

 Available for download at **resources.corwin.com/assessment-capable**

Teaching Each Other With Reciprocal Teaching

Reciprocal teaching (Palincsar & Brown, 1984) is a highly effective way to apply comprehension strategies throughout a text, and has an effect size of 0.74 (Hattie, 2009). Students read collaboratively in small groups using text that has been segmented into passages of a few paragraphs each. At each stopping point, the group has a discussion about what they have just read, using four comprehension strategies:

- Summarizing the passage for key understandings

- Posing questions about the passage

- Clarifying unfamiliar vocabulary or concepts

- Predicting what the next passage will offer in terms of information

Once students have been taught the reciprocal teaching protocol (often estimated to take a few weeks), increased attention should be placed on the nature of the discourse itself, as students take on more control.

Therefore, the role assignments that may be utilized when first learning the protocol (Summarizer, Questioner, Clarifier, Predictor) are faded in order for more natural discussions to occur. The true value of reciprocal teaching is that it affords all the members of the group a chance to teach one another, and in turn, be taught by peers.

The sixth-grade team at Nelson Mandela Academy spent the early weeks of the school year introducing and reinforcing reciprocal teaching (RT) in all of their classes. "This collaborative effort helped us spread the workload among all of us, so that we could use it all year long," explained English teacher Arief Khouri. Once the students learned about the roles and procedures of reciprocal teaching, they were able to use it more flexibly. Social studies teacher Martin Andrews routinely uses it with primary source documents featured in the textbook. "We're study-ing ancient history, and these documents are pretty archaic. They're a lot harder to understand than rest of the textbook," said Mr. Andrews. "To tell the truth, I used to skip these because when I assigned them, the kids didn't understand them. Using the RT protocol has given me a tool to assist with that." Mr. Khouri added, "What's got me stoked is that I hear my students having conversations like RT even when we're not specifically doing [the protocol]. That's proof for me that this has become a transfer skill, not just something the teacher makes you do."

Conclusion

The take-away for this chapter is that students, as assessment-capable visible learners, recognize their own learning and are able to teach one another. Of course, students have to be taught how to do so and learn what to do with the information they provide and receive. In essence, assessment-capable visible learners learn to be reflective and self-aware. They come to understand that their learning is a journey and that there are not bad places to be and that they can be further along. To develop this kind of thinking, teachers have to ensure that their students do not rely exclusively on adults for information about needed areas of additional learning or improvement. Rather, students start to rely on themselves and know how to self-assess, rather than waiting passively for their teacher to tell them when they've learned something. In other words, they're active. They want to know their status so that they can improve even further.

Assessment-capable visible learners recognize their own learning and are able to teach one another.

None of this is going to be accomplished if the tasks teachers assign are simple or lack complexity. Rich, rigorous tasks allow students an opportunity to struggle, to figure out what they still need to learn, and when they are ready to move forward. This happens when their learn-ing is visible and when they recognize that there are endless opportu-nities to learn.

MINDFRAMES OF SCHOOLS
That Create Assessment-Capable Visible Learners

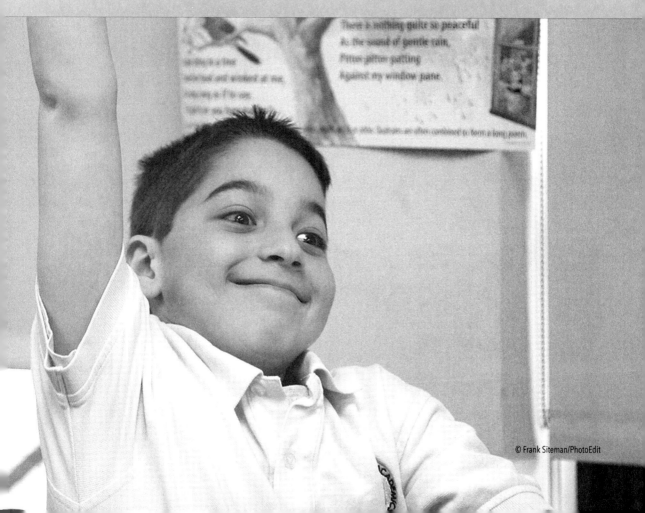

Our colleague Megan McCrary is an example of an assessment-capable teacher. She is a high school English teacher who makes sure her students understand where they are and where they're headed. Her students set goals for themselves, exercise choice, gauge their progress, and recognize next steps in their learning. As you can imagine, there is a lot of teaching, conversation, consulting, and sometimes a bit of cajoling that lies behind all of this. One tool she has developed is a unit tracking sheet so that both teacher and student can communicate about their map for learning (see Figure 8.1 on pages 138–139). We will highlight a few features that assist students in becoming more assessment capable.

Ms. McCrary provides a rationale for her students about the three-week unit of study, which focuses on themes of redemption and is designed to coincide with the schoolwide essential question, "What makes a life meaningful?" The overall design of the tracking sheet is meant to signal to students their progress toward mastery, as noted by the cumulative percentage in the right columns. Each day her students explain the lesson's learning intentions verbally, in writing, or through visuals. They engage in several tasks related to annotation, writing for argumentation, and discussion. Each student meets with the teacher after the first week to set an additional choice goal of his or her own.

The competencies themselves come toward the end of the unit, and students make decisions about the level they intend to pursue. Ms. McCrary offers three levels. The first is a simplified competency ("comp") which focuses on comprehension and analysis of unit concepts and skills. Students who select this level and pass it will earn a C, which is in the 70% to 79% range. A second option is at the master level and requires additional evaluation skills, as well as creating a new product. Students successfully achieving this level can earn at least a 90%. Given the theme of forgiveness, hope, and salvation in this unit, Ms. McCrary added an optional level component for students to deepen their learning for A-level work (effect size of service learning is 0.58). B-level work (80%–89%) is reserved for those that exceed the requirements of the simplified competency by fulfilling the service-learning extension, and for those who attempted but were not entirely successful on the master-level competency.

The English teacher noted that student decision making gives her a reason to consult with individuals:

> Sometimes I'll have a student who selects the simplified comp, and I'll say, "*But I know you can do more than that.*" Encouragement can help, but there are other times I find out that they've got an Incomplete in math and they're making time management

decisions. Sometimes I can help with that, too. You have to talk with them to find out their reasoning, and there are lots of times when they have very good reasons.

Ms. McCrary includes confidence ratings on the tracking sheet to foster self-questioning, self-monitoring, and related metacognitive thinking. Their confidence ratings allow her the opportunity to confer with students individually about their learning. These tracking sheets become a vehicle for discussion, reflection, and taking action. Her goal, of course, is to have all of her students strive for A-level work. However, her work with adolescents has shown her that choice, whether spoken or unspoken, is a crucial factor in their learning. One-on-one conferences provide her with a forum for helping students raise expectations of themselves above what it is that they believe they can do.

Her classroom is often noisy and active, with students working together in small groups, and sometimes individually. The teacher is invariably in consultation with an individual student, an accomplishment in a classroom with 40 students. When she announces, *"Stamp Town is open!"* students check their tracking sheets to determine whether it is time to check in with her.

Assessment-capable visible students are cultivated in assessment-capable schools. Consider the skills and habits assessment-capable learners bring to the equation. These students make the most of the opportunities their teachers create to fuel their own learning. These students are skilled at interpreting the data that give them an indication of where they are in their learning, and when they are ready to move forward. These assessment-capable visible learners can employ their own self-assessments and use the results to inform their future learning. The frequent feedback they get (self, peers, teacher) all strengthens their ability to estimate their own performance and make decisions about new goals. They know how to interpret their data and serve as agents in the learning of their classmates.

Of course, these students don't somehow magically appear at the classroom door, announcing their assessment-capable status. They are created by equally skilled teachers and school leaders who possess a deep understanding of what they want to see in their students. These teachers engage in competency-based grading that focuses on mastery, not compliance. Their use of formative and summative evaluation is not done simply for the purposes of measuring and ranking students but because they know that these events are designed primarily to give children a means for decision making about their own learning.

Assessment-capable schools possess the mindframes that allow students to become their own teachers because they deeply understand their own role in their learning.

Figure 8.1   Unit Tracking Sheet

Unit 5 Tracking Sheet
English 9

Unit 5 WHY: *Be aware that individuals (and perhaps the world) are capable of change, which helps us relate to and think deeply about texts and statements about life. The idea is to apply this knowledge to our actions, our life paths, and our world view.*

Unit 5 WHAT: *Scholars will analyze the idea of redemption in a variety of texts and media (to include expository/informational selections, TED Talks, documentary, etc.) and explore the complexities of forgiveness, hope, and salvation.*

Number	Date(s)	Assignment Title and Success Criteria	Progress Toward Mastery (%)	Stamp
1		**Learning Intention Collage *(Whole Class and Individual Activities)*** I can explain the Unit 5 Learning Intentions each day using both words and visuals.	10%	
2		**Essential Question Discussion and Five Words Activity *(Group and Individual)*** ***What makes a life meaningful?*** I can respond to the EQ and translate my thoughts using five words to create a sentence/idiom or list (practice word choice).	20%	
3		**Annotate Expository Text and Write Claim-Evidence-Reasoning Response *(Individual)*** I can annotate an informational text and demonstrate my understanding by completing CER earning a 90% or above.	35%	
4 (50%)		**SCHOLAR'S CHOICE *(Individual)*** I can . . . *(instructor and scholar will create this self-selected goal together.)*	50%	
Comp *Simplified* **COMPETENT** (70%)		**Unit 5 Competency #1 *(Individual)*** *Scholar must demonstrate basic competency (comprehend and analyze) of Unit 5 concepts, skills, themes, and questions to earn a C.*	70%	

Number	Date(s)	Assignment Title and Success Criteria	Progress Toward Mastery (%)	Stamp
Comp *Complex* **MASTER** (90%)		**Unit 5 Competency #2 *(Scholar's Choice)*** *Scholar must demonstrate Mastery (evaluate and create) of Unit 5 concepts, skills, themes, and questions to earn an A.*	90%	
Extension *Apply learning elsewhere/ Service learning* (100%)		**Extension Assignment *(Scholar's Choice)*** I can extend my learning and deepen my understanding of the Unit 5 concepts, themes, and questions by applying my learning in the community. *(Service Learning component)*	100%	

Success Criteria Confidence Ratings (1—*not confident at all* to 10—*super confident/CRUSHING IT, BUDDY!*)

Assignment Number	Confidence Rating (1–10)	Explanation of Confidence Rating
1		
2		
3		
4		
5		
Unit 5 Competency/ies		

Source: © Megan McCrary, Health Sciences High and Middle College Inc.

This final chapter is a call to action. Assessment-capable schools possess the mindframes that allow students to become their own teachers because they deeply understand their own role in their learning. Teachers, school leaders, and school systems play crucial parts in developing these learners. Each must seek to understand impact and make adjustments accordingly. Leaders of assessment-capable schools are knowledgeable about the value of instructional leadership in fostering the kind of teaching that makes this possible. Finally, school systems must work in concert with students, teachers, and leaders to close the opportunity-to-learn gap. This requires a focus on issues of equity, which are addressed in part through the way we structure schools so that every child can become a visible learner.

School systems must work in concert with students, teachers, and leaders to close the opportunity–to–learn gap. This requires a focus on issues of equity, which are addressed in part through the way we structure schools so that every child can become a visible learner.

Assessment-Capable Schools Are Filled With Adaptive Learning Experts

The teachers of assessment-capable visible learners are adaptive learning experts. In other words, they know the students in their class come with a unique array of strengths, talents, challenges, and knowledge gaps. However, they don't aspire to somehow get all of their students to cross the same finish line at the same moment in time. After all, uniformity is when you're producing widgets—less so when your profession is human growth. Rather, teachers of assessment-capable visible learners are in the game to maximize and accelerate human potential. Acceleration, which is the act of moving students forward at ever-increasing speed, requires momentum. Catalysts for building learning momentum include grouping strategically and flexibly and using formative and summative evaluation skillfully.

Assessment-Capable Schools Use Strategic and Flexible Grouping

Students' learning can be enhanced with lots of meaningful interactions with a broad and rich range of peers. That means that assessment-capable schools have dismantled outdated and ineffective systems that track students into learning trajectories that limit their potential. The overwhelming evidence is that tracking and ability grouping, while expensive in terms of finances and human resources, has little effect on learning, with an effect size of 0.12 (Hattie, 2009). Instead, these heterogeneous classrooms hum with lots of peer interactions with diverse gifts and abilities. However, these interactions should be structured so that students can gain the most from one another. When students are working together in small groups, the predominant arrangement is to construct these heterogeneously (mixed-ability groups). Heterogeneous grouping of large and small groups is sound for several reasons, including maintaining social relationships, fostering positive behaviors, encouraging cooperative learning, and developing student self-efficacy (Hattie, 2002). But the success of heterogeneous grouping is also linked to the teacher's high expectations and skill at using grouping flexibly. In a study of 12 elementary schools in New Zealand, teachers in the intervention group were taught about the positive effects of high expectations on student learning, how to use flexible grouping in mathematics, and how to foster choice and student decision making in learning (Rubie-Davies & Rosenthal, 2016). It should come as no surprise to readers that the students in these classrooms made meaningful gains in mathematics achievement when compared to those in the control group. These gains held whether the student was initially identified as being a low-, average-, or high-achieving student. As well, when the control group teachers received similar professional development, their students also made equivalent gains.

Video 8.1
The Characteristics of an
Assessment-Capable School

*resources.corwin.com/
assessment-capable*

Student learning is a complex stew built on relationships, motivation, expectations of self, expertise, and the beliefs of the teacher. It would be far too reductionist to say that simply putting students into heterogeneous groups and then hoping for the best would be sufficient. Skilled teachers keep all of these factors in mind as they construct groups and the tasks they will complete. Keeping a trained eye on both the knowledge development of students and their metacognitive knowledge about how they learn is key. Teachers who use flexible and heterogeneous grouping to foster learning know that bridging the gaps that might lie within a group are essential if students are to learn from one another. Fifth-grade teacher Darby Webb sometimes employs an alternate ranking system to form groups. "I list [students] according to their present level of performance. I have one list that ranks them according to their achievement on the last unit of instruction. I have another list that's based on their social and communication skills," she said.

Ms. Webb's process is to divide the list in half, then create heterogeneous groups by pairing students from each half-list (see Figure 8.2). In this example, students 1 and 2 (on the first half-list) are paired with the top two from the second half-list (17 and 18). This allows for groups to remain heterogeneous without creating too wide of a gap. Of course, teacher discretion should also be used. For instance, Leighanne and Sam have a history of conflict, so Ms. Webb adjusts by moving one of them to the next grouping. "Alternative ranking gets me thinking more carefully about how I develop groups, and having more than one list prevents me from only seeing them in terms of academic progress," said the teacher.

Figure 8.2   Alternate Ranking System Sample

1. Keisha	17. Rudolfo
2. Arturo	18. Sara

3.	19.
4.	20.
5.	21.
6.	22.

15. Leighanne	31. Felicia
16. John	32. Sam

online resources   Available for download at **resources.corwin.com/assessment-capable**

Ms. Webb also groups according to choice. "I don't always have students working on the same task simultaneously. Sometimes it's the tasks that are varied, and the students select which ones they'll complete." During a science unit on variations of traits, Ms. Webb introduced stations related to DNA expression through pea plants, a computer simulation that demonstrated how peppered moths changed over several generations due to pollution, and a reading and accompanying activity about how the beaks of finches on the Galapagos adapted over time. "They'll do all of these over the next three lessons, but giving them choice in the order they complete them allows for other grouping arrangements." Each station is equipped with tablets with questions that check for understanding. "They need to work together to answer the questions because they are all short constructed responses, not multiple choice," she explained. "However, they can't go to the next station until they have successfully addressed the writing prompt. I read the group responses and tell them if they've done so. Sometimes they don't get it the first time, so they have to put their heads together to figure it out."

> Uniformity is when you're producing widgets—less so when your profession is human growth. Rather, teachers of assessment-capable visible learners are in the game to maximize and accelerate human potential.

Assessment-capable visible learners are built from the ground up. Older students in particular have learned to rely on external entities, primarily teachers and grades, to tell them how they're doing. While these are useful information sources, they aren't sufficient. Students need to be aware of their learning and have opportunities to take action. Doing so requires assessment-capable schools.

Mindframes of Assessment-Capable Schools

Individual teachers, of course, can create assessment-capable visible learners. The teachers we have profiled throughout this book are a testament to the influence each has in making students self-aware. The words and actions of the students in this book may seem idealistic, but in fact are real kids. It's just that assessment-capable visible learners are that extraordinary. They exhibit insights and behaviors we thought had not been possible. Now think of what can be accomplished when teachers and school leaders work within systems that allow these learners to thrive. Imagine how the learning trajectory shifts, and how learning accelerates as a result. Students can flourish in school environments that allow them to lead their own learning. Doing so requires coordination of effort.

Teachers

It is very good news indeed that teachers can be such powerful influencers of student learning—we wouldn't have it any other way. To do so requires that teachers possess a mindframe that, first and foremost, appreciates one's role as being an evaluator of impact on student learning (Hattie, 2012). As noted in *Visible Learning* (2009) and *Visible Learning for Teachers* (2012), 95% of interventions work when the alternate is no learning at all. The effect sizes presented throughout this book have been demonstrated to advance student learning in ways that should cause us to take note. But none of these approaches is magical. A small dose of goodness isn't going to deliver the results you hope for. These approaches are mediated across three dimensions: frequency, intensity, and duration. No matter the potential power, any "effective" approach remains unrealized if done only occasionally, indifferently, or briefly. But even when implemented with fidelity, you may still not achieve the results you desire. That's why knowing one's impact is crucial.

Video 8.2
Mindframes of
Assessment-Capable
Teachers

resources.corwin.com/
assessment-capable

Impact

As discussed in Chapter 1, the true litmus test is the extent to which your teaching positively impacts the learning of your students. This confronts deeply held, but rarely discussed, beliefs about the relationship between teaching and learning. We have all heard teachers make the kind of "blame the student" statements that cause the rest of us to wonder if teaching is their calling at all: the secondary teacher who boasts about how many students failed his class because he's "rigorous," the elementary teacher who says "her family just doesn't care" and therefore that's why the girl doesn't achieve, the primary teacher who assumes an impoverished level of language exposure in a child's first years and therefore absolves herself from expecting much of anything at all from her student. Our role is to figure out where they are currently and then advance their learning. Without question, we all have students who are not yet achieving at expected levels. But there are two words in that last sentence that matter: *yet* and *expected*. *Not yet* means we are optimistic about their future growth. *Expected levels* says that we hold high expectations for all our students, regardless of the starting point. These teachers embrace the challenge and never settle for less. Their optimism and enthusiasm, along with their competence in their discipline, add up to their credibility in the eyes of their students. Teacher credibility goes a long way in advancing learning, with an effect size of 0.90, equivalent to two years' worth of growth for a year in school.

The overwhelming evidence is that tracking and ability grouping, while expensive in terms of finances and human resources, has little effect on learning, with an effect size of 0.12.

Teacher credibility is further enhanced through a deep understanding of one's impact on learning. The effect sizes that are cited throughout this book are extracted from huge data sets, often containing tens or hundreds of thousands of students. But you can also calculate your own effect size using formulas calculated in an Excel spreadsheet. These effect sizes can be calculated from yearly, by semester, or even quarterly. Some teachers even do them by unit just to keep tabs on progress. Further, these effect sizes can report on the growth of the entire class, or on an individual student. Administration of a pre- and postassessment is one easy way to acquire the data you need. For instance, writing samples scored on the same rubric at different points in the year can track progress of your students and provide you with feedback about the impact of your teaching on their learning. The calculations themselves require several steps once the data have been entered into the spreadsheet. A simple and informative six-minute video on how to calculate group and individual effect sizes can be found at https://vimeo.com/51258028.

We needn't be afraid to look, but rather need to cultivate a belief about the usefulness of feedback to ourselves about the processes we are using. If in fact we believe that feedback is critical for students to forward their learning, why would it not be the same for ourselves? Further, we can model for our students the kind of reflective thinking, goal setting, and monitoring we value in them by discussing our own data. Assessment-capable visible learners need to be apprenticed into these metacognitive habits by witnessing it regularly in the people who are instrumental to their learning lives—their teachers.

School Leaders

School leaders can play an essential role in the learning lives of students, especially when they see themselves as instructional leaders (Robinson, Lloyd, & Rowe, 2008). This identity is critical for school improvement efforts to succeed, as the overwhelming evidence worldwide is that the variance within a school is greater than the variance between schools (Schmidt, Burroughs, Zoido, & Houang, 2015). But addressing the professional needs of teachers requires more than just seeking to instill a single instructional model for everyone to follow. As with students, we need to look at teacher growth, not simply compliance, as our standard operating procedure. We will draw a comparison to school accountability models. The first is a status model, while the second is a growth model. Status models have been rightly criticized because they start with the false assumption that all schools somehow are interchangeable and occupy a level playing field. We know that's not the case, as schools face a variety of challenges and strengths within the communities they serve. A growth model, on the other hand, holds high expectations as a constant, but sets goals that describe steady progress and a positive trajectory. School leaders and instructional coaches foster assessment-capable teachers by changing the conversation toward a growth model. In doing so, we talk much more about learning, and a bit less about teaching. That means that classroom observations focus on what students are saying and doing, not just what the adult in the front of the room said or did. Instructional leaders look down, not just up, to gain insight into what is occurring and use these insights to prompt dialogue and mediate the thinking of teachers. They ask, "Why do you think that is so?" rather than saying, "Here's what I think you should do."

The assessment data that we receive—benchmarks as well as summative evaluations—serve as feedback to ourselves as leaders about what we have done and not done yet. Don't step into the act of blaming others. We caution teachers not to externalize and rationalize how students are letting us down. We can't suddenly use the same faulty logic to project blame on teachers without also reflecting on our own effectiveness. Again, model what you want to see in others. Assessment-capable school leaders share their goals and discuss their own progress. They discuss the strategic thinking they utilize to resolve problems. They say, "I want to be mindful of how I interpret data as feedback to me as well as you," rather than, "Here's what this data mean. How are you going to fix it?"

And just as positive relationships between students and teachers matter, so do those among the adults at the school. It is difficult to imagine how sustainable any model is when the output far exceeds the input. Yet teachers are often asked to do that every day, all day long. Teachers are expected to be endlessly patient and positive, to be sensitive and responsive to the needs of their students, and to guide the learning of others. But if we fail to do the same for them, they will soon be drained of all they have. Purkey (1991) discussed the idea of education through invitation, noting that the most effective teachers are inviting to their

Video 8.3
Mindframes of
School Leaders

resources.corwin.com/
assessment-capable

students. Inviting teachers foster trust and respect, exhibit optimism, and do so in ways that display their overt intentionality. In contrast, uninviting teachers hold low expectations, have a low sense of self-efficacy, and are pessimistic. How did they get that way? Perhaps they lack the self-perception to analyze their impact. And perhaps they themselves have rarely felt the invitation to the work. School leaders can be intentionally inviting, too, displaying a level of optimism about the staff and working intentionally to build trust and respect.

Assessment-capable visible learners need to be apprenticed into these metacognitive habits by witnessing it regularly in the people who are instrumental to their learning lives—their teachers.

Systems

Working together, teachers and school leaders develop systems for ensuring the development of assessment-capable visible learners. The first place they look, quite critically, is in the master schedule for the school. Equity lives in the master schedule, as it dramatically influences the opportunities to learn that students often experience differentially (Schmidt et al., 2015). Schools should eliminate the expensive but ineffective practice of tracking and ability grouping students ($d = 0.12$), as the results show "minimal effects on learning outcomes and profound negative equity effects" (Hattie, 2009, p. 90). Students in lower tracked classes rarely advance to a higher track, as they receive less challenging course work and fall further behind other classmates with each passing year—if for no other reason than they are not offered the curriculum exposure that allows them ever to catch up and move upward! Tracking, despite decades of research, is alive and well. According to the 2009 National Assessment of Educational Progress (NAEP) survey of principals, the most frequently tracked courses were those in mathematics. However, the variance was startling. Arkansas had the lowest rate of tracking at 50%, while Nevada had the highest at 97%. We can assume the variance isn't due to substantially different students in these two states, but rather the relative capacity to address the problem. In contrast, the country of Finland, long held in esteem for its excellent educational results, does not begin tracking until the age of 16, after students have completed their basic education and now select whether to pursue an academic or vocational track (Sahlberg,

QUESTIONS FOR REFLECTION

Based on the criteria provided in Chapter 8, where is your school on the journey of becoming an assessment-capable school?

2014). Ability grouping of students identified as gifted isn't much stronger, with an effect size of 0.30. In the meantime, the true cost lies in the damage done to identity and agency within a system that reinforces low expectations for some students. Is it any wonder that so many low-achieving students willfully leave our high schools before graduation? And many middle school educators and school leaders will tell you that the process of dropping out begins years earlier as students disengage from school.

The second practice that should be slated for elimination is in-grade retention. With an effect size of -0.13, it represents a learning *loss*, as any early academic gains have disappeared within two years or so (Hattie, 2009). If you are skeptical of this, we invite you to find out how students at your school who were retained five years ago are doing now. If they are thriving, then perhaps your retention efforts are effective after all. But if they're not, you must change what is being done in the name of helping children.

One of the problems related to in-grade retention is that repeating the grade becomes the only intervention. Assessment-capable systems move to action, replacing retention with active intervention. The student-level processes outlined in this book—setting goals, acquiring strategies, gauging progress, and so on—mirror response to intervention practices (RTI). The effect size of RTI, which is fueled by feedback, data, and a focus on impact, is robust at 1.09, representing more than two years' worth of growth for a year in school (Hattie, 2009). For students already demonstrating early failure, what makes more sense? Doing the same thing a second time, or committing to an intensive search for what works for this child?

A final practice assessment-capable schools can enact is to commit to the business of using the language of learning, especially with parents. Make sure that systems have been developed to more fully involve parents in their child's learning. We don't mean volunteering to trim laminated posters in the workroom, but rather getting them involved in the learning conversation with their children. An assessment-capable visible learner who can speak about her progress with her teacher should be able to do so with her family. Student-led conferences with their families change the formula, as the teacher plays a supporting role in the discussion. As you educate yourselves about the importance of impact, educate families as well. They have tremendous influence over the learning lives of their children. Figure 8.3 lists the mindframes of teachers and school leaders who work together to create assessment-capable schools.

Video 8.4

Culture and Climate at Assessment-Capable Schools

resources.corwin.com/ assessment-capable

Figure 8.3   Mindframes of Teachers and School Leaders

1. Teachers and school leaders believe their fundamental task is to evaluate the impact of their teaching on student learning.

2. Teachers and school leaders believe that success and failure in student learning is about what they did or did not do.

3. Teachers and school leaders talk more about the learning than the teaching.

4. Teachers and school leaders see assessment as feedback about their impact.

5. Teachers and school leaders engage in dialogue, not monologue.

6. Teachers and school leaders enjoy the challenge and never retreat to "doing their best."

7. Teachers and school leaders believe it is their role to develop positive relationships with students and staff.

8. Teachers and school leaders inform all about the language of learning.

Source: Hattie, J. (2012). *Visible learning for teachers: Maximizing impact on learning.* New York, NY: Routledge. Used with permission.

Conclusion

Assessment-capable visible learners possess the skill and the will that allow them to become their own teachers. They have learned *how*, not just what, to learn. But these students will languish in a fallow field without the cultivating skills of teachers, school leaders, and school systems. They are dependent on us to show them the way. This book has been about developing these assessment-capable visible learners, who

We caution teachers not to externalize and rationalize how students are letting us down. We can't suddenly use the same faulty logic to project blame on teachers without also reflecting on our own effectiveness.

- Know their current level of understanding (Chapter 2)

- Understand where they're going and have the confidence to take on the challenge (Chapter 3)

- Select tools to guide their learning (Chapter 4)

- Seek feedback and recognize that errors are opportunities to learn (Chapter 5)

- Monitor progress and adjust their learning (Chapter 6)

- Recognize their learning and teach others (Chapter 7)

We can't help but draw some parallels to what parents do. A difficult fact new parents must confront is that one day their children will reach adulthood and leave them. Therefore, a major job parents have from the earliest years of their children's lives is to prepare them to leave. As teachers we must confront the fact that in most cases our students will only be with us for a single school year. Therefore, we must prepare them from the first days of the school year to leave us. It isn't just detailing what they should know, but how they can become increasingly assessment capable so they can fuel their own learning. As school leaders and school systems, we must do all we can to support teachers' endeavors in accomplishing this goal. Assessment-capable visible learners are "future proof" because they are ready for anything the world may hand them.

QUESTIONS
FOR
REFLECTION

Think about some of the approaches you have implemented or plan to implement. Consider the dimensions of frequency, intensity, and duration.

How might you influence student learning in the most meaningful way?

REFERENCES

Absolum, M., Flockton, L., Hattie, J., Hipkins, R., & Reid, I. (2009). *Directions for assessment in New Zealand (DANZ): Developing students' assessment capabilities.* Wellington, New Zealand: Ministry of Education.

Adesope, O. O., Trevisan, D. A., & Sundararajan, N. (2017). Rethinking the use of tests: A meta-analysis of practice testing. *Review of Educational Research, 87*(3), 659–701.

Almarode, J., Fisher, D., Frey, N., & Hattie, J. (2018). *Visible learning for science, grades K–12: What works best to optimize student learning.* Thousand Oaks, CA: Sage.

Almeda, V., Baker, R., & Corbett, A. (2017). Help avoidance: When students should seek help, and the consequences of failing to do so. *Teachers College Record, 119*(3), 1–24.

Bandura, A. (1997). *Self-efficacy: The exercise of control.* New York, NY: W. H. Freeman.

Baumann, J. F., Jones, L. A., & Seifert-Kessell, N. (1993). Using think alouds to enhance children's comprehension monitoring abilities. *The Reading Teacher, 47*, 184–193.

Berger, R., Rugen, L., & Woodfin, L. (2014). *Leaders of their own learning: Transforming schools through student-engaged assessment.* San Francisco, CA: Jossey-Bass.

Biggs, J. (1999). *Teaching for quality learning at university.* Buckingham, England: Society for Research into Higher Education and Open University Press.

Boekaerts, M. (1997). Self-regulated learning: A new concept embraced by researchers, policy makers, educators, teachers, and students. *Learning and Instruction, 7*, 161–186.

Bong, M. (2013). Self-efficacy. In J. Hattie & E. M. Anderman (Eds.), *International guide to student achievement* (pp. 64–66). New York, NY: Routledge.

Bransford, J. D., Brown, A. L., & Cocking, R. R. (Eds.). (2000). *How people learn: Brain, mind, experience, and school.* Committee on Developments in the Science of Learning and Committee on Learning Research and Educational Practice. Washington, DC: National Academy Press.

Brookhart, S. M. (2008). *How to give effective feedback to your students.* Alexandria, VA: ASCD.

Bulgren, J. A., Schumaker, J. B., & Deshler, D. D. (1997). *The concept anchoring routine.* Lawrence, KS: Edge Enterprises.

Butler, R. (1998). Determinants of help seeking: Relations between perceived reasons for classroom help-avoidance and help-seeking behaviors in an experimental context. *Journal of Educational Psychology, 90*, 630–643.

Butler, R., & Shibaz, L. (2014). Striving to connect and striving to learn: Influences of relational and mastery goals for teaching on teacher behaviors and student interest and help seeking. *International Journal of Educational Research, 65,* 41–53.

Caprara, G., Fida, R., Vecchione, M., Del Bove, G., Vecchio, G., Barabaranelli, C., & Bandura, A. (2008). Longitudinal analysis of the role of perceived self-efficacy for self-regulatory learning in academic continuance and achievement. *Journal of Educational Psychology, 100*(3), 525–534.

Cazden, C. B. (1988). *Classroom discourse: The language of teaching and learning.* Portsmouth, NH: Heinemann.

Chi, M. T. H. (2000). Self-explaining expository texts: The dual processes of generating inferences and repairing mental models. In R. Glaser (Ed.), *Advances in instructional psychology: Educational design and cognitive science* (pp. 161–238). Hillsdale, NJ: Erlbaum.

Clark, A. M., Anderson, R. C., Kuo, L., Kim, I. H., Archodidou, A., & Nguyen-Jahiel, K. (2003). Collaborative reasoning: Expanding ways for children to talk and think in school. *Educational Psychology Review, 15*(2), 181–198.

Clarke, S., & Hattie, J. (forthcoming). *Feedback: The visible learning story.* Abingdon, England: Routledge.

Claxton, G., & Lucas, B. (2016). The hole in the heart of education (and the role of psychology in addressing it). *The Psychology of Education Review, 40*(1), 4–12.

Daeun, P., Gunderson, E. A., Eli, T., Levine, S. C., & Beilock, S. B. (2016). Young children's motivational frameworks and math achievement: Relation to teacher-reported instructional practices, but not teacher theory of intelligence. *Journal of Educational Psychology, 108*(3), 300–313.

Davey, B. (1983). Thinking aloud—modeling the cognitive processes of reading comprehension. *Journal of Reading, 27,* 44–47.

Dingath, C., Buetter, G., & Langfeldt, H. P. (2008). How can primary school students learn self-regulated learning strategies most effectively? A meta-analysis on self-regulation training programmes. *Educational Research Review, 3,* 101–129.

Donohoo, J. (2017). *Collective efficacy: How educators' beliefs impact student learning.* Thousand Oaks, CA: Corwin.

Dweck, C. S. (2007). *Mindset: The new psychology of success.* New York, NY: Ballantine Books.

Dweck, C. S. (2016). Praise the effort, not the outcome? Think again. *TES: Times Educational Supplement,* (5182), 38–39.

Ericsson, K. A., Krampe, R. T., & Tesch-Römer, C. (1993). The role of deliberate practice in the acquisition of expert performance. *Psychological Review, 100,* 363–406.

Evans, M. A., Williamson, K., & Pursoo, T. (2008). Preschoolers' attention to print during shared book reading. *Scientific Studies of Reading, 12*(1), 106–129.

Fendick, F. (1990). *The correlation between teacher clarity of communication and student achievement gain: A meta-analysis* (Unpublished doctoral dissertation). University of Florida, Gainesville.

Ferlazzo, L. (2010, June 16). My revised final exams (and an important lesson). *Larry Ferlazzo's websites of the day.* Retrieved from http://larryferlazzo.edublogs.org/2010/06/16/my-revised-final-exams

Finn, A. N., Schrodt, P., Witt, P. L., Elledge, N., Jernberg, K. A., & Larson, L. M. (2009). A meta-analytical review of teacher credibility and its associations with teacher behaviors and student outcomes. *Communication Education, 58*(4), 516–537.

Fisher, D., & Frey, N. (2007). *Scaffolded writing instruction*. New York, NY: Scholastic.

Fisher, D., & Frey, N. (2011). *The purposeful classroom: How to structure lessons with learning goals in mind*. Alexandria, VA: ASCD.

Fisher, D., & Frey, N. (2014). *Better learning for structured teaching: A framework for the gradual release of responsibility* (2nd ed.). Alexandria, VA: ASCD.

Fisher, D., & Frey, N. (2015). *Checking for understanding: Formative assessment techniques for your classroom* (2nd ed.). Alexandria, VA: ASCD.

Fisher, D., Frey, N., & Hattie, J. (2016). *Visible learning for literacy*. Thousand Oaks, CA: Corwin.

Fisher, D., Frey, N., & Hattie, J. (2017). *Teaching literacy in the visible learning classroom, grades K–5*. Thousand Oaks, CA: Corwin.

Fisher, D., Frey, N., & Pumpian, I. (2011). No penalties for practice. *Educational Leadership, 69*(3), 46–51.

Flavell, J. H. (1985). *Cognitive development*. Englewood Cliffs, NJ: Prentice Hall.

Frey, N., & Fisher, D. (2013). *Rigorous reading: Five access points for helping students comprehend complex texts, K–12*. Thousand Oaks, CA: Corwin.

Gross-Loh, C. (2016, December 16). How praise became a consolation prize. *The Atlantic*. Retrieved from https://www.theatlantic.com/education/archive/2016/12/how-praise-became-a-consolation-prize/510845

Hattie, J. (2002). Classroom composition and peer effects. *International Journal of Educational Research, 37*, 449–481.

Hattie, J. (2009). *Visible learning: A synthesis of over 800 meta-analyses relating to achievement*. New York, NY: Routledge.

Hattie, J. (2011). Feedback in schools. In R. M. Sutton, M. J. Hornsby, & K. M. Douglas (Eds.), *Feedback: The communication of praise, criticism, and advice* (pp. 265–278). New York, NY: Peter Lang.

Hattie, J. (2012). *Visible learning for teachers: Maximizing impact on learning*. New York, NY: Routledge.

Hattie, J. (2017). *Misinterpreting the growth mindset: Why we're doing students a disservice* [Web log post]. Education Week. Retrieved from http://blogs.edweek.org/edweek/finding_common_ground/2017/06/misinterpreting_the_growth_mindset_why_were_doing_students_a_disservice.html

Hattie, J., & Donoghue, G. M. (2016). Learning strategies: A synthesis and conceptual model. *Science of Learning, 1*. doi:10.1038/npjscilearn2016

Hattie, J., Fisher, D., & Frey, N. (2016). *Visible learning for literacy: Implementing the practices that work best to accelerate student learning*. Thousand Oaks, CA: Corwin.

Hattie, J., Fisher, D., Frey, N., Gojak, L. M., Moore, S. D., & Mellman, W. (2017). *Visible learning for mathematics: What works best to optimize student learning*. Thousand Oaks, CA: Corwin.

Hoover, J. J., & Patton, P. R. (1995). *Teaching students with learning problems to use study skills: A teacher's guide*. Austin, TX: Pro-Ed.

Kapur, M. (2016). Examining productive failure, productive success, unproductive failure, and unproductive success in learning. *Educational Psychologist, 51*(2), 289–299.

King, A. (1992). Facilitating elaborative learning through guided student-generated questioning. *Educational Psychologist, 27*(11), 111–126.

Kruger, J., & Dunning, D. (1999). Unskilled and unaware of it: How difficulties in recognizing one's own incompetence lead to inflated self-assessments. *Journal of Personality and Social Psychology, 77*(6), 1121–1134.

Laal, M., & Ghodsi, S. M. (2012). Benefits of collaborative learning. *Procedia: Social and Behavioral Sciences, 31*, 486–490.

LaBerge, D., & Samuels, S. J. (1974). Toward a theory of automatic information processing in reading. *Cognitive Psychology, 6*(2), 293–323.

Lee, J., & Yoon, S. Y. (2017). The effects of repeated reading on reading fluency for students with reading disabilities: A meta-analysis. *Journal of Learning Disabilities, 50*(2), 213–224.

Martin, A. J. (2006). Personal bests (PBs): A proposed multidimensional model and empirical analysis. *British Journal of Educational Psychology, 76*(4), 803–825.

Martin, A. J. (2013). Goal orientation. In J. Hattie & E. M. Anderman (Eds.), *International guide to student achievement* (pp. 353–355). New York, NY: Routledge.

Martin, A. J., Marsh, H. W., & Debus, R. L. (2003). Self-handicapping and defensive pessimism: A model of self-protection from a longitudinal perspective. *Contemporary Educational Psychology, 28*(1), 1–36.

Martinez, M., Roser, N., & Strecker, S. (1998). "I never thought I could be a star": A readers theatre ticket to fluency. *Reading Teacher, 52*(4), 326–334.

Marton, F., & Säljö, R. (1976). On qualitative differences in learning—1:Outcome and process. *British Journal of Educational Psychology, 46*(1), 4–11.

Michaels, S., O'Connor, C., & Resnick, L. (2008). Deliberative discourse idealized and realized: Accountable Talk in the classroom and in civic life. *Studies in Philosophy and Education, 27*(4), 283–297.

Morris, A. (1995). *Houses and homes.* New York, NY: Scholastic.

Munter, C., Stein, M. K., & Smith, M. S. (2015). Dialogic and direct instruction: Two distinct models of mathematics instruction and the debate(s) surrounding them. *Teachers College Record, 117*(11), 1–32.

Nathan, M. J., & Petrosino, A. (2003). Expert blind spot among preservice teachers. *American Educational Research Journal, 40*(4), 905–928.

Ogle, D. M. (1986). K-W-L: A teaching model that develops active reading of expository text. *The Reading Teacher, 39*(6), 564–570.

Palincsar, A. S., & Brown, A. (1984). Reciprocal teaching of comprehension-fostering and comprehension-monitoring activities. *Cognition and Instruction, 1*(2), 117–175.

Paris, S. G., Lipson, M., & Wixson, K. (1983). Becoming a strategic reader. *Contemporary Educational Psychology, 8,* 293–316.

Pauk, W. (1962). *How to study in college.* Boston, MA: Houghton Mifflin.

Pauk, W., & Owens, R. J. Q. (2011). *How to study in college.* Boston, MA: Wadsworth Cengage Learning.

Pintrich, P. R., & De Groot, E. V. (1990). Motivational and self-regulated learning components of classroom academic performance. *Journal of Educational Psychology, 82,* 3.

Purkey, W. W. (1991). *What is invitational education and how does it work?* Paper presented at the 9th annual California State Conference on Self-Esteem, Santa Clara, CA. 3–40.

Reinholz, D. L. (2015). Peer-assisted reflection: A design-based intervention for improving success in calculus. *International Journal of Research in Undergraduate Mathematics Education. 1,* 234–267.

Renaud, R. D. (2013). Attitudes and dispositions. In J. Hattie & E. M. Anderman (Eds.), *International guide to student achievement* (pp. 57–58). New York, NY: Routledge.

Ritchhart, R., Church, M., & Morrison, K. (2011). *Making thinking visible: How to promote engagement, understanding, and independence for all learners.* San Francisco, CA: Jossey-Bass.

Robinson, V., Lloyd, C., & Rowe, K. (2008). The impact of leadership on student outcomes: An analysis of the differential effects of leadership types. *Educational Administration Quarterly, 44,* 635–674.

Ross, D., Fisher, D., & Frey, N. (2009). The art of argumentation. *Science and Children, 47*(3), 28–31.

Rubie-Davies, C., & Rosenthal, R. (2016). Intervening in teachers' expectations: A random effects meta-analytic approach to examining the effectiveness of an intervention. *Learning & Individual Differences, 50,* 83–92.

Sadler, P. M., & Good, E. (2006). The impact of self- and peer-grading on student learning. *Educational Assessment, 11*(1), 1–31.

Sahlberg, P. (2014). *Finnish lessons 2.0: What can the world learn from educational change in Finland?* (2nd ed.). New York, NY: Teachers College Press.

Samuels, S. J. (1979). The method of repeated readings. *The Reading Teacher, 32*(4), 403–408.

Schmidt, W. H., Burroughs, N. A., Zoido, P., & Houang, R. T. (2015). The role of schooling in perpetuating educational inequality. *Educational Researcher, 44*(7), 371–386.

Schoenfeld, A. H. (1992). Learning to think mathematically: Problem-solving, metacognition, and sense-making in mathematics. In D. Grouws (Ed.), *Handbook for research in mathematics teaching and learning* (pp. 334–370). New York, NY: Macmillan.

Schunk, D. H. (2012). *Learning theories: An educational perspective* (6th ed.). Boston, MA: Pearson.

Svenson, O. (1981). Are we all less risky and more skillful than our fellow drivers? *Acta Psychologica, 47*(2), 143–148.

Sztajn, P., Confrey, J., Wilson, P. H., & Edgington, C. (2012). Learning trajectory based instruction: Toward a theory of teaching. *Educational Researcher, 41*(5), 147–156.

Taylor, W. L. (1953). Cloze procedure: A new tool for measuring readability. *Journalism and Mass Communication Quarterly, 30*(4), 415–433.

Templeton, S. (2003). The spelling/meaning connection. *Voices from the Middle, 10*(3), 56–57.

Therrien, W. J. (2004). Fluency and comprehension gains as a result of repeated reading: A meta-analysis. *Remedial & Special Education, 25*(4), 252–261.

Voerman, L. A., Meijer, P., Korthagen, F., & Simons, R. P. (2012). Types and frequencies of feedback interventions in classroom interaction in secondary education. *Teaching & Teacher Education, 28*(8), 1107–1115.

Willingham, D. T. (2003). *How to help students see when their knowledge is superficial or incomplete.* American Federation of Teachers. Retrieved from https://www.aft.org/periodical/american-educator/winter-2003-2004/how-help-students-see-when-their-knowledge

Zhang, J., & Stahl, K. A. D. (2011). Collaborative reasoning: Language-rich discussions for English learners. *Reading Teacher, 65*(4), 257–260.

Zohar, A., & David, A. B. (2009). Paving a clear path in a thick forest: A conceptual analysis of a metacognitive component. *Metacognition Learning, 4*(3), 177–195.

Zumbrunn, S., Ekholm, E., Stringer, J. S., McKnight, K. M., & DeBusk-Lane, M. D. (2017). Student experiences with writing: Taking the temperature of the classroom. *Reading Teacher, 70*(6), 667–677.

Zumbrunn, S., Marrs, S., & Mewborn, C. (2016). Toward a better understanding of student perceptions of writing feedback: A mixed methods study. *Reading & Writing, 29*(2), 349–370.

Literature Cited

Adler, D. A. (2004). *Cam Jansen and the mystery of the stolen diamonds*. New York, NY: Puffin.

Alexander, K. (2017). *The playbook: 52 rules to aim, shoot, and score in this game called life*. New York, NY: HMH Books for Young Readers.

Anaya, R. (1994). *Bless me, Ultima*. New York, NY: Warner.

Beaty, A. (2013). *Rosie Revere, engineer*. New York, NY: Harry N. Abrams.

Berne, J. (2013). *On a beam of light*. San Francisco, CA: Chronicle.

Diamond, J. (1999). *Guns, germs, and steel: The fates of human societies*. New York, NY: W. W. Norton.

Haddix, M. P. (2000). *Among the hidden*. New York, NY: Simon & Schuster.

Littman, S. D. (2016). *Backlash*. New York, NY: Scholastic.

Palacio, R. J. (2012). *Wonder*. New York, NY: Alfred A. Knopf.

Sandburg, C. (1918). *Cornhuskers*. New York, NY: Henry Holt.

Sobel, D. J. (2007). *Encyclopedia Brown, boy detective*. New York, NY: Puffin.

Telgemeier, R. (2010). *Smile*. New York, NY: Scholastic Graphix.

Thomas, A. (2017). *The hate u give*. New York, NY: HarperCollins.

INDEX

**Douglas Fisher,
Nancy Frey,
John Hattie**

Ensure students demonstrate more than a year's worth of learning during a school year by implementing the right literacy practice at the right moment.

**Douglas Fisher,
Nancy Frey,
John Hattie,
Marisol Thayre**

High-impact strategies to use for all you teach— all in one place. Deliver sustained, comprehensive literacy experiences each day.

**John Almarode,
Douglas Fisher,
Nancy Frey,
John Hattie**

Learn the precise instructional approach to use at each phase of the learning cycle— surface, deep, and transfer—for maximum-impact science teaching.

**John Hattie,
Douglas Fisher,
Nancy Frey,
Linda M. Gojak,
Sara Delano Moore,
William Mellman**

By incorporating John Hattie's ground-breaking analysis and common mathematics research, you will have the tools to design powerful, precision learning.

**Nancy Frey,
Douglas Fisher,
Molly Katherine Ness,
Kristine Michele Allen**

By strengthening foundational metacognitive skills, these learner's notebooks guide students to understand what they're learning, why they're learning it, and the strategies they need along the way. These notebooks are available for learners in Grades K–2, 3–5, 6–8, and 9–12, and are accompanied by a facilitator's guide.

CORWIN
A SAGE Publishing Company

CORWIN HAS ONE MISSION: to enhance education through intentional professional learning.

We build long-term relationships with our authors, educators, clients, and associations who partner with us to develop and continuously improve the best evidence-based practices that establish and support lifelong learning.